GREAT HISPANIC-AMERICANS

CONSULTANT:
NICOLÁS KANELLOS, PH.D.

CONTRIBUTING WRITERS:
ROBERT RODRIGUEZ
TAMRA ORR

  Publications International, Ltd.

CONTRIBUTING WRITERS:

Robert Rodriguez is a freelance writer specializing in history and pop culture. He was a contributor to *The Sixties Chronicle* and is the author of *The 1950s' Most Wanted: The Top 10 Book of Rock & Roll Rebels, Cold War Crises, and All American Oddities*. He lives with his wife and son in Elmhurst, Illinois.

Tamra Orr is a full-time, award-winning writer living in the Pacific Northwest. She has written almost 50 nonfiction books, including *Ronald Reagan: Portrait of an American Hero, Alan Shepard: The First American in Space, Sally Ride: The First American Woman in Space,* and *Violence in Our Schools: Halls of Hope, Halls of Fear,* as well as countless magazine articles.

Contents

Contents

THE HISPANIC-AMERICAN LEGACY

Hispanic-Americans have provided a stirring but sometimes overlooked background of accomplishments and contributions to the making of this nation. Great Hispanic-Americans is not meant to be a Hispanic-American hall of fame but is a collection of luminaries taken from all walks of life in an effort to reveal how Latinos of today and yesterday have contributed to U.S. society.

HISPANIC HISTORY IN North America began some 500 years ago. It is a collective history of the individuals who first ranched cattle in Florida, introduced the metal plow and planted cotton in Texas, spun wool and wove it into blankets in New Mexico, created irrigation systems for the arid lands of the Southwest, and innovated mining techniques in Arizona. Although their names are lost forever, these innovators are the ancestors of today's Hispanic-Americans or Latinos. What must never be forgotten is that the advancement of American civilization has been built on the solid base of Latino contributions throughout our history.

Latinos were founding the first towns and churches in Puerto Rico, before the arrival of the Mayflower. They were involved in the first translations and transcriptions of Native-American languages and religious beliefs in what became Georgia and the planting of the first wine grapes in California. You can see from the first underground railroad for escaped slaves, and the first free black communi-

ties, that Latino achievement was on track to provide a basis for our pluralistic society, in blending the races and contributions of the peoples of Europe, Africa, and the Americas. From the fertile soil of the Latino past, a Hispanic-American culture is part of our national identity; Latinos are finally allowed their rightful place in the media, entertainment, and, most importantly, the national consciousness.

Each of these biographies, while revealing a distinct and particular story, also represents the commonalities of our experience, values, and ideals: the fierce determination of immigrants to cross oceans and rivers and deserts to build a successful life once opportunity is at hand; the perseverance to bridge the grand divides of language and education and social class; the willingness to

Educator Jaime Escalante turned the fortunes of his inner-city high school students around by promoting high standards of scholarship and adding calculus to their math curriculum.

Above: **Activist César Chávez first gained prominence in championing rights for migrant workers in the Southwest and eventually became an icon for labor reform nationwide.** *Right:* **Judith Baca went from painting in the back of her elementary school classroom to becoming a world-renowned muralist.**

share what little they have with those perceived as less fortunate; the desire to learn the lessons of the elders and to become role models for the youth; and the need to respect, honor, and preserve family and community. Finally, these short profiles illuminate the drive of individuals to achieve great distinction, not so much in their own names but in the names of their community and their culture.

One constant in Latino culture has always been our focus on the family and the community. In this spirit, these biographies are presented as valuable examples of where we as a people have come from and how we contribute to the

community and national life. Out of our past, we can highlight our collective struggle for dignity and equality, as exemplified by such individuals as labor leaders Dolores Huerta and César Chávez of the United Farm Workers union or civil rights leader Raúl Yzaguirre of the National Council of La Raza. Foreshadowing the height of today's artistic achievement in the novels of Isabel Allende and Oscar Hijuelos, the art of Judith Baca and Luis Jiménez, the acting of Rita Moreno and Martin Sheen, and the plays and films of Luis Valdez, in the not-so-distant past were the elegant verses of José Martí, the incisive prose of María Amparo Ruiz de Burton, the philosophy of Félix Varela and George Santayana, the mid-19th century itinerant theater companies and, before them, the architecturally ageless Southwestern missions. From 19th-century carters, printers and publishers,

ties or through awareness of our historical imperatives in this land.

Great Hispanic-Americans, thus, is meant to be more than a collection of biographies, more than a gallery of heroes. This is our collective narrative on how to succeed by contributing to the community, to the nation, to humankind. Among our selected biographies are those of the very famous, such as Mario Molina, the Nobel laureate, and Ellen Ochoa, the astronaut; however, also included are the not-so-famous whose names may once again be lost to posterity. It is their achievement, their contribution that matters to us more than their names. Each of them invites you to engage in the pursuit of excellence, not to bask in the light of fame nor celebrity but in continuity and within the spirit of our selfless desire to leave this world a better place than we found it.

Nicolás Kanellos

Brown Foundation Professor of Hispanic Literature, University of Houston Founding Director, Arte Público Press

imporaters and exporters, our business and trade missions have grown into mighty corporations led by the likes of Joseph Unanue and Roberto Goizueta. Historians and educators such as Carlos E. Casteñeda and Américo Paredes from the early part of the 20th century demonstrated the importance of presenting knowledge to future generations, an idea given practice today by Jaime Escalante and Antonia Pantoja. All of these achievers, past and present—whether the children of untold generations in their native United States of America or recent arrivals as immigrants or political refugees seeking greater opportunity and freedom—acknowledge their success as having been facilitated by others in their families and communi-

Oscar Hijuelos made history when his book *The Mambo Kings Play Songs of Love* became the first novel by a Hispanic-American to win a Pulitzer Prize for fiction.

ISABEL ALLENDE

Raised in a world of diplomats, Isabel Allende has written best-selling books that entertain and educate people from all cultures and generations. She has taken everything life has handed her and turned it into a body of stories that reaches out and touches the reader's heart.

Isabel Allende started writing *The House of the Spirits* on January 8, 1981, the day she learned her beloved grandfather was dying. "I began a letter for him that later became my first novel," she once explained. The book was a best seller the world over.

ALTHOUGH MOST OF Isabel Allende's books are works of fiction, they carry a great deal of truth from her own life experiences. Her father was a Chilean diplomat stationed in Lima, Peru, where Allende was born. Her parents divorced when she was three, and she accompanied her mother in returning to Chile. Allende's mother later married another diplomat, so the family did a great deal of traveling.

As a young woman, Allende held several jobs, including secretary at the United Nations, host of a local Santiago, Chile, television show, editor of a children's magazine, and writer at a feminist magazine. In 1962, she married an engineer named Miguel Frías. Her cousin Salvador Allende was a rising socialist politician in Chile during the 1960s. When he was elected president of Chile in 1970, Isabel Allende worried that family members might be kidnapped for political reasons. That fear was the inspiration for her first play, *The Ambassador*.

Things changed dramatically in 1973 with the military takeover of the Chilean government and the violent death of President Allende. Shocked by these events, Isabel Allende spoke out—a perilous act in that volatile climate. Her next two years were filled with increasingly dangerous activities: helping hunted citizens reach foreign embassies, passing on vital information, and providing food to the families of kidnapping victims. By 1975, Allende and her family were receiving death threats. They left their homeland for Venezuela, where they remained for 13 years.

In Venezuela, Allende wrote her first novel, *The House of the Spirits*. To her surprise, it received a wonderful international reception, as did her second novel, *Of Love and Shadows*. After her third book, she became a full-time writer. "I spend ten, twelve hours a day alone in a room writing. I don't talk to anybody; I don't answer the telephone. I'm just a medium or an instrument of something that is happening beyond me, voices that talk through me. I'm creating a world that is fiction but that doesn't belong to me."

Over the next several years, Allende continued to write rich, deep stories, and by 1987, she was the most-read female Latin-American novelist in the world. Now divorced, she traveled to the United States in 1988 to promote her books. There she met one of her biggest fans: a lawyer named William Gordon—her future husband.

In 1991, Allende wrote a nonfiction book on a painfully personal topic: the death of her daughter, Paula. "When I was writing *Paula*, my assistant would come to the office and find me crying. She would hug me and say, 'You don't have to write this.' And I would say, 'I am crying because I am healing. Writing is my way of mourning.' That book was written with tears, but . . . very healing tears. After it was finished, I felt that my daughter was alive in my heart, her memory preserved."

Since finishing *Paula*, Allende has authored more novels, such as *Daughter of Fortune* and *Portrait in Sepia*; the cookbook *Aphrodite: A Memoir of the Senses*; the memoir *My Invented Country*; and a trilogy for young adults. She always starts every book she writes on January 8— the day she began her very first novel long ago.

Allende has described her enduring bond with her mother, Francisca Llona Barros, as the longest love affair of her life. Panchita Llona, as she is known familiarly, was responsible for many of the recipes that appeared in *Aphrodite: A Memoir of the Senses*.

LUIS WALTER ALVAREZ

*Winner of the Nobel Prize in Physics, Luis Walter Alvarez explored everything
from subatomic particles to how the dinosaurs really became extinct.
His heritage led him to science, but his passion for the field kept him there.*

IT WAS NO SURPRISE when Luis Alvarez became a scientist—it was in his blood. His grandfather had come to the United States from Cuba in the 1870s and was a doctor for the kingdom of Hawaii. Alvarez's father, Walter Alvarez, was a medical doctor at the Mayo Clinic who wrote a popular newspaper column about health and became known as "America's Family Doctor."

Luis Alvarez was fascinated by machines and tools from an early age. By 11, he could build circuits and crystal radios. Summers during high school were spent learning about instruments from the machinists at the Mayo Clinic. That interest stayed with him throughout his life and led him to discoveries and history-altering research. In 1928, Alvarez attended the University of Chicago and, taking a class in advanced experimental physics, proclaimed "love at first sight." Eight years later, Alvarez graduated with a Ph.D. in physics. He began teaching at the University of California at Berkeley but was pulled away by the government to go to the Massachusetts Institute of Technology (MIT) Radiation Laboratory, where he made advances in radar technology.

In 1944, Alvarez went to New Mexico's Los Alamos Scientific Laboratory to work on the atomic bomb. He created a detonation device for the bomb that was dropped on Hiroshima. Later, he flew over the devastation, and while he found

Winner of the Noble Prize in Physics, Luis Alvarez allowed his intellectual curiosity to lead him into other areas, such as geology and government service. Throughout his career, Alvarez also received the Collier Trophy from the National Aeronautical Association, the Medal for Merit, the Einstein Medal, and the National Medal of Science.

it upsetting, he felt his country had made the right decision. In a letter to his four-year-old son, he wrote, "What regrets I have about being a party to killing and maiming thousands of Japanese civilians this morning are tempered with the hope that this terrible weapon we have created may bring the countries of the world together and prevent future wars."

During the five years he worked for the government, Alvarez developed machines called bubble chambers in order to study atomic particles. He was able to detect, record, and analyze 70 different particles. This research led directly to his winning the Nobel Prize in Physics in 1968.

After World War II, Alvarez returned to Berkeley for another 20 years of experimentation and research. His coworkers referred to him as the "prize wild idea man." His influence went beyond the campus borders, however, as demonstrated by his service on the Warren Commission, which investigated the assassination of President John F.

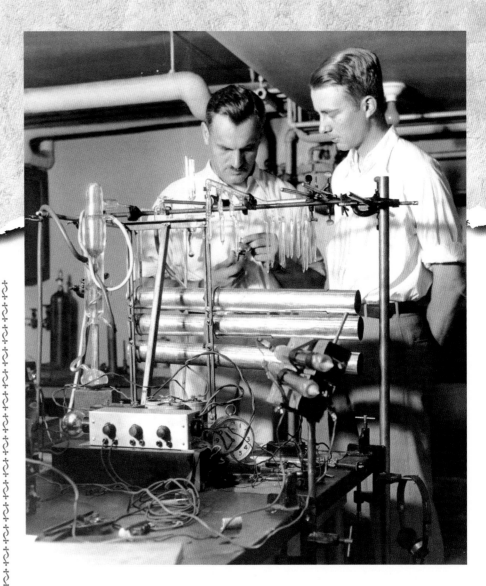

Kennedy. In 1980, Alvarez and his geologist son Walter came up with the "impact theory" to explain why dinosaurs became extinct. They came to the conclusion that a giant asteroid had hit Earth, throwing so much dust into the stratosphere that the sky was pitch black for years. Plants died and eventually most animals, including the dinosaurs, starved to death. By the time of his death in 1988, Alvarez held 22 patents, only part of the scientific legacy he left behind.

In this 1933 photograph, Alvarez, a student at the University of Chicago, works with his graduate advisor, Nobel Laureate Arthur Compton. Under Compton, Alvarez conducted research about cosmic rays.

DESI ARNAZ

Having led a life that went from riches to rags and back again, actor and musician Desi Arnaz is sometimes remembered as "Mr. Lucille Ball," but it was his own business savvy and instinctive ingenuity that made him the incredible success that he was.

Desi Arnaz captured the hearts of many television viewers as the always straight, often flustered, and quite lovable Ricky Ricardo. He managed to put up with a zany red-headed wife week after week and, in the process, changed how America perceived Hispanics.

DESIDERIO ALBERTO ARNAZ y de Acha III had it pretty good. His youth in Santiago, Cuba, was split between his family's three ranches, their city home, and a vacation home on a private island. This wealthy lifestyle came to an abrupt end in 1933, however, when the Cuban government was overthrown and the Arnaz family lost everything. They fled to Miami, Florida, and a completely different way of life.

Arnaz found himself working odd jobs, such as cleaning bird cages and driving trucks and taxis. But in 1934, he became guitarist for a Cuban band. During one performance, he was approached by Spanish rumba king Xavier Cugat, who asked Arnaz to sing with his famous orchestra. Arnaz toured with them for a year and then returned to Miami to start his own band. It was perfect timing. Latin-American music was in, and dances such as the samba and bossa nova filled dance floors. When Arnaz introduced the conga in 1938, it became the number one dance craze.

From there, his fame only increased. In 1939, he starred in the Broadway musical *Too Many Girls* and recreated his role on film the following year. His movie costar was actress Lucille Ball. Less than a year later, the two were married.

The next decade was hectic. Arnaz, traveling with his band, saw little of his movie-making wife. He also starred in several films himself, including *Father Takes a Wife* and *Bataan*. In 1943, he was inducted into the U.S. Army, where he entertained the troops.

In an attempt to spend more time together in 1950, Arnaz and Ball wanted to produce and star in a half-hour television comedy. Although CBS desired Ball, network executives balked at casting Arnaz as her husband, claiming such a relationship unbelievable. To convince the network of the show's viability, Arnaz and Ball formed their own production company, Desilu, and filmed a pilot episode. This impressed CBS, and *I Love Lucy* was born. America adored

Left: **Desi Arnaz and Lucille Ball take a stroll together around Desilu Studios. Desilu became one of the most powerful television studios in Hollywood, producing a number of memorable TV series.** *Above:* **The fictional Ricardo family was featured on many different magazine covers during the 1950s. On this cover of *Look* for December 25, 1956, Ball and Arnaz pose with Keith Thibodeaux, who played their son Little Ricky on *I Love Lucy.***

that were filmed out of order and then edited together, *I Love Lucy* was filmed in three consecutive acts with three separate cameras. Arnaz also obtained the rights to every episode after it was broadcast and, two years later, sold the reruns back to CBS for more than $4 million. Desilu Studios became the largest studio in the country, producing such TV hits as *The Untouchables*, *Star Trek*, and *Mission: Impossible*.

After ten years, *I Love Lucy* came to an end and so did Arnaz and Ball's marriage. Although he claimed to retire in 1962, Arnaz remained quite productive. He remarried, owned a horse breeding farm, and wrote his autobiography. He kept his hand in show business, starring in *The Escape Artist*, producing a situation comedy called *The Mothers-in-Law*, and even hosting an early *Saturday Night Live*. He died in 1986 of lung cancer.

the show, and Arnaz's character, Ricky Ricardo, gave the nation a new perspective on Hispanics.

I Love Lucy changed how television was produced. While most TV shows were produced on the East Coast, Arnaz shot *I Love Lucy* in California. He demanded a live audience, a first for situation comedies, and invented the three act/three camera technique. Unlike other programs

JUDITH BACA

Struggling as a Spanish speaker in an English-language school system, Judith Baca discovered her artistic calling by accident. By combining her talents with her personal concerns for multicultural youth, she has created art that is bigger than life!

Judy Baca intends her art to reach beyond herself, to bring the community together, and to connect it all to a greater purpose and meaning.

WHEN JUDITH FRANCISCA BACA attended elementary school, she encountered a real problem. Born in south central Los Angeles, she had grown up speaking Spanish and struggled to follow her lessons in an English-speaking school. To help her pass the day, she was allowed to paint in the back of the room and in the process discovered her passion for art. "My mother says—and I know very well—my earliest memory of art-making has to do with my...entrance into school, in kindergarten, being a child that spoke very little English," she once recalled. Explaining further, she said, "It was really against the rules to speak Spanish, and I was really freaked-out, you know. But I *loved* painting.... They very often would let me paint...instead of doing some of the other lessons, because I didn't speak English well enough. So I had a lot of painting."

Baca continued to love art throughout Catholic high school and California State University at Northridge. Her first large public project was a mural on a city wall in Los Angeles's Hollenbeck Park. To help paint the mural, she enlisted the help of city youth from a variety of street gangs. With brushes in their hands and a goal in front of them, the kids temporarily forgot their differences and worked together. Baca combined her passion for art with her concerns for street youth and the discrimination many of them encountered daily.

Hired by the city of Los Angeles, Baca became a roving art teacher, moving from place to place teaching art and creating murals. She also traveled to Mexico to learn more about the mural art form from some of that country's most famous muralists. In 1976, she started work on "The Great Wall of Los Angeles" in the

This is a small section of "The Great Wall of Los Angeles," the world's longest mural. Full of vibrant colors, the piece encompasses the history of ethnic groups that affected California from prehistoric times through the middle of the 20th century.

Tujunga Wash Flood Control Channel. The project, 2,435 feet long, illustrates the history of ethnic groups and cultures and their contributions to California. It took seven years to complete. The crew that worked on it was immense, including 40 scholars, 40 artists, 100 support staff, and more than 400 multicultural community youths between the ages of 14 and 21.

Baca followed that project with a more international one in 1987, "The World Wall," subtitled "A Vision of the Future Without Fear." This mural was painted on seven 10×30-foot panels designed to fit together in a circle 100 feet in diameter. It portrayed many issues near and dear to Baca's heart, including war, peace, cooperation, interdependence, and spiritual growth. The 210 feet of portable panels toured the world.

Today, Baca's work is exhibited nationally and internationally, at the Smithsonian and other museums. Her commissioned mural "La Memoria de Nuestra Tierra," or "Our Land Has Memory," appears at the Denver International Airport. Since 1996, Baca has served as vice-chair of UCLA's César E. Chávez Center and professor of art in the university's department of world arts and cultures. Her work is a testament to ethnic heritage and the power of people working together.

JOAN BAEZ

Music fans recognize Joan Baez for her pure, clear soprano voice and folk ballads, but history will focus most on her dedication to human rights and the plight of those who cannot speak for themselves.

Above: Joan Baez was in the forefront of activism and music during the 1960s and has remained active in both fields ever since. *Right:* Baez was shocked at the success of her first album and how quickly her life changed, as her new career required constant touring.

WHEN DR. ALBERTO VINICIO BAEZ took his daughter to a Boston coffeehouse, he had little idea that it would eventually put her on a career pathway to fame. As the two sat down, performers on the small stage began to sing a folk ballad, and young Joan Chandos Baez was captivated. The woman called the "Queen of Folk Music" and the "Godmother of Modern Folk" had just seen her future in the songs.

Born in Staten Island, New York, Baez moved frequently with her family, living in California and even Baghdad, Iraq, for a short time. After Baez graduated from high school, the family moved to the Boston area so Dr. Baez could teach at the Massachusetts Institute of Technology.

After Baez's initial exposure to folk music, she got a guitar and began learning ballads. Her amazingly beautiful voice allowed her to play in local coffee-

houses. A record promoter spotted her and booked her into the premier Chicago folk club, The Gate of Horn. There she met a singer named Bob Gibson, who invited her to appear with him at the first Newport Folk Festival in Rhode Island in 1959. The crowd loved the 18-year-old. The next year, she appeared there again, solo this time, and record companies began courting her. Baez chose Vanguard Records, and in November 1960, *Joan Baez* was released. The record was a huge success and was followed by many others as Baez's fame and popularity grew. She was one of the many performers at the historic Woodstock concert in 1969.

Even as Baez kept recording, her interests were shifting. As a child she had endured racial discrimination for her Hispanic looks, and now she wanted to help others who were being persecuted. In 1962, Baez appeared on the

rights demonstrations; opposing the Vietnam War; supporting gay rights; and advocating the nuclear freeze movement. In addition to singing at countless benefits for these causes, she visited war-torn countries, carried picket signs, and made speeches. She has joined and established multiple human rights organizations and has won more than a dozen awards from these groups. Baez holds two honorary degrees in Humane Letters from Antioch and Rutgers universities.

Baez has had eight gold albums, one gold single, and six Grammy nominations. She continues to record, tour, and support political causes. Her entire life has been about helping, and as she says, "You don't get to choose how you're going to die. Or when. You can decide how you're going to live now."

cover of *Time* magazine, not for her music but for her involvement in civil rights issues. As she put it, "My concern has always been for the people who are victimized, unable to speak for themselves and who need outside help."

Over her lifetime, she has worked intensely to improve a number of political issues, including helping Hispanic farm workers in California; working to desegregate southern college campuses; marching with Martin Luther King, Jr., in civil

LUCREZIA BORI

To aficionados, opera is imbued with a passion and sublime artistry that raises it to among humanity's highest pursuits. For fans throughout the early 20th century, one of the biggest and most accomplished opera stars was soprano Lucrezia Bori.

Spanish-born diva Lucrezia Bori was the first Hispanic opera star of the 20th Century.

BORN IN VALENCIA, SPAIN, Lucrezia y Borja Gonzales de Riancho discovered her gift for song early. Her parents saw to her musical education at the local conservatory, and as her skills progressed, she was sent to Milan for further study. This put her among the cream of the music world, where Bori's delicate phrasings, as well as her powerful presence, drew notice.

In 1908 at the age of 21, Bori made her professional debut in *Carmen* at Rome's Teatro Adriano. She played Micaela, the gentle ingénue in Georges Bizet's tale of a tragic love triangle. The acclaim she received for the performance kept her services in demand throughout Italy. In San Carlo, she was pegged as a worthy substitute for the popular Maria Farneti in Puccini's *Madam Butterfly*. For a relative newcomer, this was a real coup.

Soon, her intense yet soulful vocal stylings drew notice from the profession's musical heavyweights. The most coveted role a soprano could desire in 1910 was that of the title character in another Puccini work, *Manon Lescaut.* New York's renowned Metropolitan Opera, appearing in Paris at the time, had assigned a popular but undependable diva to the production. Realizing the error with the opening just weeks away, the opera company frantically sought a replacement. It received recommendations for Bori, and a private audition was set up in Milan. In attendance were famed conductor Arturo Toscanini and composer Giacomo Puccini himself.

Lucrezia Bori's fragile beauty and compelling charisma made her a natural, but it was the command she had over her voice that carried the day. At turns forceful, subdued, and elegant, her superb and instinctive use of her instrument won them over. She debuted in Paris with the traveling Metropolitan opposite the great tenor Enrico Caruso. Although invited to perform with the Metropolitan in New York, Bori instead honed her craft under a two-year contract at La Scala in Milan, Italy.

ordering Bori to rest her voice indefinitely. For nearly two years, she did not utter a sound. But while hiking one day, a startle produced a tiny gasp—the surgery had worked. Extensive therapy followed, and in 1921 she made a triumphant return to the Met stage.

In 1912, however, she made her long-awaited New York premier. Reprising the part in which she'd wowed Parisian audiences, her performance marked the beginning of a decades-long association with the Met that would continue long after her singing days were over.

The next few years saw her go from strength to strength, but the price of success was overwork. Nodes were detected on her vocal chords in 1915, a potentially career-ending malady. Following an unsuccessful initial surgery, doctors who had treated Caruso performed a second operation, this time

For the remainder of her performance career, she found adoration in a variety of roles, but most especially with Puccini's work. Her fans ranged from heads of state to somewhat less likely notables: a Prohibition-era performance near Chicago saw the cast saluted with a case of real champagne, courtesy of admirer Al Capone.

Bori retired from performing in 1936 but remained on the Met's board of directors. Her success and popularity would prove inspirational to later generations of Hispanic aspirants, including Tatiana Troyanos and Verónica Villarroel.

This 1928 New York Metropolitan Opera performance featured Bori opposite Beniamino Gigli in Puccini's *La Rondine*. Bori was a favorite of the composer, giving definitive portrayals of many of his heroines.

ALBERTO CALDERÓN

Known the world over for his mathematical formulas, Alberto Calderón was one of the most influential scholars of the 20th century. He created a school of thinking that is still studied today.

BORN IN MENDOZA, Argentina, Alberto Calderón spent the majority of his life working with mathematical theories and formulas that most people could not begin to grasp then or now. Unlike other mathematicians of his time, he did not focus on abstract mathematical concepts but instead turned his attention to practical equations that could be applied to help analyze physical functions. Most of his study was focused on the development of concepts that are crucial to functions such as heat conduction and sound transmission.

Calderón's early school years were spent in his hometown and in Zuk, Switzerland. He graduated from the University of Buenos Aires in 1947 with a degree in civil engineering. Three years later, he completed work on his doctorate at the University of Chicago. During one special session with Professor Antoni Zygmund, Calderón proposed that the solution to a class problem was already written in the teacher's text, an idea Zygmund refuted. Calderón didn't real-

ize he had solved the problem more efficiently than his professor had.

After this, the two mathematicians formed a relationship as mentor and student and eventually became partners. Together, they created the Calderón-Zygmund theory of singular integral operators. They were also the inspiration for the "Chicago school of analysis," which is still taught in many universities. Colleague Robert Fefferman stated that the Calderón-Zygmund theory was "unquestionably one of the most important developments in analysis in the 20th century." Felix Browder, former vice president of Rutgers University, said Calderón "was one of the most original and profound mathematical analysts of the past 50 years."

After Calderón obtained his Ph.D., he taught at Ohio State University; the Institute for Advanced Study in Princeton, New Jersey; and the Massachusetts Institute of Technology. He returned to the University of Chicago in 1959,

received many awards and honors, including the Bocher Memorial Prize and the Steele Prize, both from the American Mathematical Society, and the Wolf Prize, one of the highest awards given in mathematics. In 1991, President George H. W. Bush presented him with the National Medal of Science for "ground-breaking work on singular integral operators, leading to their application to important problems in partial differential equations."

Calderón died in 1998. His theories and equations continue to be used today as part of current aerodynamic engineering and even quantum physics research. His work and its seemingly infinite possibilities remain his legacy.

where he stayed for the remainder of his career. From time to time, he also returned to his native Argentina to teach at his alma mater, where he was an honorary professor. When he was there, he encouraged and even sponsored Latin-American students to pursue science degrees.

Over his lifetime, Calderón wrote more than 75 scientific papers and delivered countless lectures all over the world. He

CARLOS EDUARDO CASTAÑEDA

Carlos Eduardo Castañeda's magnum opus was a seven-volume history of the Catholic Church in Texas, published in the 1930s. Had he stuck to his original plan, the world might have been denied this extraordinary scholarship. The resulting document of his people's culture set an academic standard that remains paramount to this day.

Carlos Eduardo Castañeda chronicled the history of the Roman Catholic Church in Texas almost single-handedly with his epic 1937 work, *Our Catholic History in Texas: 1519–1936,* which has remained the bedrock for all further research on the subject.

CARLOS EDUARDO CASTAÑEDA, his parents' seventh child, was born in Ciudad Camargo, Tamaulipas, Mexico, in 1896. His family settled in Texas when he was ten. His parents' death led him to pursue a degree in civil engineering when he entered the University of Texas in 1917. This seemed a reasonable decision, given the responsibility upon him to help support his sisters, but in his third year, he felt the calling that led to his life's work. A bibliophile at heart, Castañeda discovered that switching majors to history would enable him to indulge the bliss he felt by immersing himself in antique data. At last, Castañeda had found his path.

Following graduation, Castañeda found work as a high school Spanish teacher. Once he'd completed his master's degree, he accepted a post as associate professor at the College of William and Mary in Virginia. But distance from his beloved Texas soon drew him back. In 1927, he returned to Austin, where he was named librarian of the University of Texas's Genaro García Collection of Latin-American materials. The resources entrusted to him would yield a wealth of information, all of which he put to good use. One key discovery he made was that of a dusty Mexican manuscript originally written by an 18th-century Spanish priest named Juan Augustín Morfi. Father Morfi's *History of Texas* became the subject of Castañeda's doctoral dissertation in 1935. Translated and annotated, the piece paved the way for his later masterwork.

The hard times of the Great Depression in the 1930s tended to bring out the worst in humanity, as nearly everyone struggled for economic survival. In communities where differing cultures came into contact, demonization of "the other" led to unrest, suspicion, and outright hostility. Being Mexican-born and a Catholic at a time and place where tolerance was strained put Castañeda's faith to the test. Rather than buckle under, he decided to assert his social identification by working on a study tracing the path

In 1928, Casteñeda published *The Mexican Side of the Texan Revolution,* compiling and translating material from many of the Mexican participants in Texas's war for independence. Here, the historian delivers an address at the site of the decisive 1836 Battle of San Jacinto.

of pride for the multitudes of Hispanic Catholics who felt that their culture had been given short shrift in relating the story of Texas.

Castañeda's public life was not limited to academia. In the midst of World War II, he was regional director of President Franklin Roosevelt's Committee on Fair Employment Practices. Throughout his career, Castañeda was the recipient of many honors, including a knighthood from the Equestrian Order of the Holy Sepulchre of Jerusalem and the Spanish Government's Knight Commander of the Order of Isabel La Católica in 1950. A lifelong pursuit of learning and study, centered on his church and his culture, amassed a body of scholarly data that would provide future historians with much to examine for years to come. Castañeda died in 1958.

of the Catholic Church as it shaped Texas throughout the centuries.

The resulting chronicle, released in 1937, was entitled *Our Catholic Heritage in Texas: 1519–1936.* Produced with the support of the Texas Knights of Columbus Historical Commission, Castañeda's study sought to restore the Latin role in forming Texas heritage, an element too often neglected or marginalized. Castañeda's monumental work, which he later updated to 1950, served as a source

CÉSAR CHÁVEZ

A charismatic civil rights leader, César Chávez brought the plight of migrant farm workers in the Southwest to national attention during the 1960s and 1970s. Through his efforts, conditions in which field laborers toiled saw dramatic improvement.

Through his relentless activism on behalf of migrant workers, labor leader César Chávez became a legend throughout the Mexican-American community.

CÉSAR ESTRADA CHÁVEZ was born in 1927 near Yuma, Arizona, the eldest son of six children. His parents were first-generation Mexican-Americans. Librado Chávez did well as a farmer and store owner until his son's tenth year, when, in the midst of the Great Depression and a southwestern drought, the family's fortunes were turned upside down.

A neighbor had struck a business deal with the elder Chávez but had left him high and dry. The resulting shortfall caused the Chávez farm to be seized for back taxes. The family was left with no choice but to pack up its belongings and join the thousands headed to California to pursue a livelihood as produce pickers.

This nomadic existence meant constant interruption of the children's education by long stretches in the fields. But for Librado Chávez and his family, the migrant experience also came with a rude welcome to a life of exploitation. It took them some time to learn that when they were not being ill-used in general, some

unscrupulous contractors would fleece them completely. Other difficulties included back-breaking shifts without rest, poor housing with inadequate sanitation, and slave wages as compensation for their efforts. Given a steady stream of cheap labor, growers were in no hurry to do the right thing by their employees.

With Jim Crow laws flourishing throughout much of the South, it should be no surprise that discrimination against Mexicans was codified throughout the Southwest, including California. This meant separate facilities for schooling, dining, even watching movies at the theater. Such was the world into which César Chávez came of age in the early 1940s. After a stint in the Navy during World War II, he married his sweetheart, Helen Fabela. The couple settled in a barrio called Sal Si Puedes, which means "Get out if you can."

Chávez found that World War II had done nothing to soften the attitudes of growers toward laborers. He witnessed

The soft-spoken yet charismatic César Chávez was instrumental in drawing national attention to the plight of the migrant farm worker. Here, he is seen in New York, addressing a group of supporters during the 1969 grape boycott.

the continued indifference and lack of care afforded the migrants. Attempts to address the workers' concerns fell on deaf ears, but Chávez was determined to find a way to advance their cause.

Two men he came to know were instrumental in helping shape his path. The first was Father Donald McDonnell, a scholarly member of the clergy who belonged to the local mission. He steered Chávez to the writings of Pope Leo XIII, who spoke of every person's right to equal wages and happiness. Chávez broadened his reading and was similarly affected by the words and example of Mahatma Gandhi, whose unshakable pacifism in the face of overwhelming odds forwarded a righteous cause.

The second man to influence Chávez directly was Fred Ross, leader of the Community Service Organization (CSO), a group formed to help the economically depressed Hispanics help themselves. Impressed with Chávez's drive, charm, and quiet wisdom, Ross put him to work organizing chapters of the organization throughout the state.

Chávez's efforts paid off with CSO chapters forming throughout California and Arizona. The group's strength and numbers made it an effective agent for change. Recognizing that a powerful organization was required to fight the entrenched agribusiness lobby, Chávez worked the political process, registering thousands of voters and throwing support behind candidates friendly to their interests. Small victories were claimed, but overall improvements came slowly.

A turning point came when Chávez became aware of a troubling situation in Oxnard, California. Local farm workers were being denied employment, with positions being filled by underpaid *braceros*, or Mexican nationals. Chávez organized the workers to file complaints with the California Farm Workers Service daily, hoping that the force of numbers would make them impossible to ignore. After more than 1,000 complaints, a Labor Department inspector stepped in, forcing growers to hire the local workers.

However, once the inspectors left, the locals were again replaced with the *braceros*. This cycle was repeated numerous times until Chávez organized a march

Huelga, **the word for** *strike* **in Spanish, became a rallying cry for Chávez and the farm laborers he represented.**

by farm workers on the fields, bringing along reporters to document the chicanery. The resulting press attention forced an investigation of the Farm Placement Service, which revealed bribes paid by farm owners to keep the cheap labor in place. Resignations resulted, and the CSO scored a major triumph.

Unfortunately, Chávez's ambitions to further the organization's success were met with resistance from the more conservative elements within. Undeterred, he resigned his position with the group. Taking a job pruning trees, Chávez used every other waking hour to travel the breadth of California, visiting farms and recruiting workers to join his new National Farm Workers Association.

When the National Labor Relations Act was passed in 1935, farm workers were conspicuously excluded from the right to collective bargaining accorded to those in other lines of work. Though performing a high-demand service in keeping the flow of produce coming to the nation's stores, migrant workers were routinely treated as something less than human by the business concerns running the industry. Little heed was paid to their lengthy hours in extreme conditions, injuries were common in the absence of safety precautions, and the lack of close inspections kept workers subject to the whims of their employers or contractors.

Chávez saw the need for a major corrective to these deplorable conditions, but there would be great resistance, not only from industry but from some workers themselves, who feared making trouble would only cause them to lose their jobs. Chávez knew that his choice of tactics could mean the difference between winning or losing public support, a key element to achieving victory.

One particular trouble spot involved California grape growers. In the early 1960s, long-simmering concerns finally came to a head. This highly profitable industry, accustomed to routine neglect of its field employees, was confronted by angry workers. Faced with the threat of a crippling strike, which could lead to grapes rotting on the vine, two major vineyards ultimately complied. Others did not, using the time-honored tactic of bringing in *braceros*.

Seeing the need to throw a spotlight on their struggle, Chávez switched strategies. He organized a drive to bring wider, even national pressure to bear on the situation, calling for a nationwide boycott of California table grapes. To bring further attention to the plight of farm workers, he led a 340-mile march to the California state capitol in Sacramento. The farm workers' cause was unwittingly aided by their opponent's use of strong-arm tactics, as violent confrontations ended with the beating of farm laborers. Chávez's adherence to the nonviolent principles espoused by Gandhi and Dr. Martin Luther King, Jr., served his cause well, drawing outrage toward the industry from observers. The struggle took on a spiritual dimension as well, as Chávez himself went on a 25-day fast to draw attention to the cause.

Five years later, the campaign ended with grape growers acceding to the workers' demands. Field workers were at last accorded the pay and benefits enjoyed in other industries. The plan would be utilized with similar results for lettuce growers in the 1970s.

In 1972, the organization Chávez founded was reorganized as the United Farm Workers of America. Chávez continued in his remaining years to fight on behalf of the downtrodden, adhering to his principles while using considerable tact, fairness, and common sense to achieve his aims. The measure of his success in rewriting policy to the benefit of so many without a voice was in time recognized. On August 8, 1994, more than a year after Chávez's death, President Bill Clinton presented him with a posthumous Presidential Medal of Freedom. Six years later, California Governor Gray Davis signed a bill making César Chávez's birthday a state holiday.

Among the many ways Chávez's legacy has been honored is by having schools named for him, such as this one in San Francisco. Several murals decorate the building, including this depiction of children using sign language.

SANDRA CISNEROS

Novelist and poet Sandra Cisneros adds her unique voice and experience to literature, providing a point of view that has largely been missing from the aesthetic conversation: that of the Latina with one foot in both Mexican and American cultures.

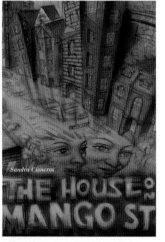

The House on Mango Street, seen here in a rare first edition, brought Sandra Cisneros into literary prominence. The book, initially released by the nonprofit Hispanic publisher Arte Público Press, found many admirers and was eventually reissued by Random House. It received an American Book Award from the Before Columbus Foundation in 1985.

SANDRA CISNEROS'S MOTHER was a Mexican-American and her father a Mexican. She grew up shuttling from Chicago to Mexico and back whenever her father grew homesick. Even in Chicago, the family moved a lot, "always in neighborhoods that appeared like France after World War II—empty lots and burned-out buildings," she once remembered. Being the only daughter alongside six sons added to her difficulties, with Sandra feeling her every move scrutinized and judged by her "seven fathers." Never comfortable in moving from school to school, the timid girl turned inward, finding escape through reading. Lewis Carroll was a particular favorite, and his mixture of imaginative poems and fantasy stories made a profound impression on Cisneros, who felt moved to express herself with creative writing.

Her introspection and soft-spoken nature became valuable as she found herself studying people and events around her. Cisneros also developed a fascination with words, both Spanish and English.

Sometimes just the look of a written word would suggest something to her, an unrealized thought or perspective, and she felt bound to put it to use. But her belief in her own talent was lacking, as she felt expectations to measure up to an "Anglo" standard of literary merit she believed was beyond her capabilities.

Following her B.A. from Chicago's Loyola University in 1976, Cisneros went to the University of Iowa for an M.F.A. There she had the revelation that changed her life. It had never occurred to her that, as a woman and a Mexican-American, her perspective was unique. She began to draw upon the deep well of her life experiences: her unsettled childhood, her sense of displacement, her alienation from her peers. This in and of itself might have been a rich enough source of material, but she added to it a layer of language merging, using Spanish words and phrases in her English poetry and prose, that created a singular tapestry of wordplay that spoke to an audience that had previously been scarcely acknowledged.

The first product of her epiphany was *The House on Mango Street* (1983). Cisneros invented a series of vignettes based on events she had observed or imagined and wove them into a novelistic structure. The book veers from funny to serious, from outrageous to deeply moving. Its use of simple but poetic language has an authenticity to the text.

Reviews were largely positive, but a more rewarding response came when schools began adding the novel to their curricula. Its freewheeling style made it attractive to adolescents turned off by conventional literature. Despite her success, however, doubts about her own abilities plagued Cisneros, paralyzing her muse. This changed when a literary agent (and fan of the book) brought her to the attention of mainstream publishers in New York, which resulted in the publication of the collection *Woman Hollering Creek and Other Stories*. This gave Cisneros the confidence she needed to take her craft to the next level.

Cisneros's career has continued to flourish, boosted by National Education Association grants and guest professorships around the country. In 2002, she published *Caramelo,* a vibrant novel depicting several generations of a Mexican-American family, to international acclaim.

Left: After years spent in the artistic wilderness, this aspiring writer discovered her voice, a unique encapsulation of the American Latina experience. Her essays and novels captivated audiences, filling a void in both female and Hispanic literatures. *Above:* In 2002, Cisneros followed up the success of her previous works with *Caramelo.* This novel tells of the experiences of three generations of an extended Mexican-American family in the United States and their mother country.

JESÚS COLÓN

An articulate and passionate author, Jesús Colón wrote about social justice, anticolonialism, democracy, and racism. A pioneer of Puerto Rican literature, he has been an inspiration to many Hispanic writers.

One of the earliest writers to describe the Puerto Rican experience on the U.S. mainland, Jesús Colón broke literary ground that continues to be harvested today.

A TEENAGE STOWAWAY on the SS *Carolina*, Jesús Colón arrived in Brooklyn in 1918. Of African descent, he was born in Cayey, Puerto Rico, and as a child lived with his family behind a cigar factory. Every day, he would listen to the local readers who stood inside the factory reading news and political information aloud to all of the workers. Without realizing it, Colón began developing a political point of view that would drive him to put pen to paper when he arrived in New York.

Although Colón wanted to write professionally, he had to supplement his passion with a variety of jobs, such as hotel porter, dishwasher, post office clerk, and stevedore. By the early 1920s, he was writing for several Spanish-language newspapers in New York, as well as *Justicia*, a socialist paper in Puerto Rico. Over the next few years, he composed local-color sketches that allowed him to serve as a kind of conscience for the Puerto Rican and Latino communities, as well as poems, literary pieces, and stories. In "Bitter Sugar: Why Puerto Ricans Leave Home," Colón wrote, "I didn't find any bed of roses in the United States. I found poor pay, long hours, terrible working conditions. I met discrimination even in the slums and in the low-paying factories where the bosses very dexterously pitted Italians against Puerto Ricans against American Negroes and Jews."

Colón wrote a column for the Communist newspaper *The Daily Worker* that was later collected into a book, *A Puerto*

Great Hispanic-Americans

30

Rican in New York and Other Sketches, published in 1961. There he wrote, "The first thing we must realize is that the Puerto Ricans have been exploited for hundreds of years.... This has been done many times with the forceful and openly criminal way of the pirate.... In one of those pirates' assaults around the middle of the 17th century, the bells of the cathedral in San Juan, Puerto Rico, were stolen and sold by one of their buccaneer ships in a little town known as New Amsterdam.... So, in the words of one of my Puerto Rican friends, when one of those 200-percent Americans ask us why do Puerto Ricans have to come to New York? We can answer: 'We come to take our bells back.'"

One of Colón's most ambitious endeavors was to start his own small press, *Editorial Hispanica*, which published books on history and politics, literary works by Hispanic authors, and translations of multiple English works on socialism into Spanish. Colón also co-authored a book on vocational education that was published after his death in 1974 by the U.S. Department of Health, Education, and Welfare.

In addition to writing, Colón dedicated a good portion of his life to politics. In 1952, he ran for state senator in New York, and in 1969, he ran for city comptroller of New York City, both times on the Communist ticket. Despite losing both races, he remained politically active and took part in various strikes and protests, especially with the American Labor Party. His example, as a writer and an activist, continues to be potent today.

Although Colón may have received far less public attention than his writing deserved, his essays have nonetheless had a major impact on how Puerto Ricans are perceived in the United States.

MIRIAM COLÓN

*As a founder and the artistic director of the Puerto Rican Traveling Theater,
Miriam Colón has helped raise the profile of many Hispanic playwrights and performers.
Her own performances in movies and on television have been seen by millions.*

Actress Miriam Colón has starred in a variety of television, stage, and screen roles since the 1950s. She is seen here in a 1962 appearance on TV's *Alfred Hitchcock Presents*.

TO LEGIONS OF movie fans, Miriam Colón was Mama Montana, the only character bold enough to stand up to Al Pacino's Tony in 1983's *Scarface*. Others may know her for her performances in a pair of long-running daytime soap operas. She also has extensive stage credits. But her most significant contribution to the arts has been through the Puerto Rican Traveling Theater.

Miriam Colón was born in Ponce, Puerto Rico. While still a youngster, she developed an interest in theater, landing her first part in a school production when she was 11. The dean of the drama department from the University of Puerto Rico was in attendance and was quite impressed with the young thespian. He allowed her to audit classes at the university, where she eventually earned a place in the school's acting troupe.

Once her considerable acting skills became evident, it was clear that the prodigy would be better served in developing her talent where it could best be nurtured. Young Colón went to New York in the 1950s accompanied by her mother, who found work as a seamstress to support her daughter's dream. Colón was quickly accepted at the famous Actor's Studio run by Elia Kazan, placing her in the company of the many legends who had passed through its doors, including James Dean and Marilyn Monroe. At 17, Colón debuted on Broadway, opposite some of the finest talent of the 1950s.

She soon discovered, however, that choice roles for Latinas were hard to come by. Rather than accept parts as domestics or heavies, she found work in an array of off-Broadway shows, such as a Spanish-language production of the Puerto Rican classic *La Carreta (The Oxcart)*. Her work in the play *Me, Candido!* first took her west. Following the show's run in New York, she reprised the role in Los Angeles. This placed her in proximity to Hollywood, where she soon became a fixture guesting on several television series, mostly westerns.

After her first noteworthy speaking part on the big screen in Marlon Brando's 1961 directorial debut, *One-Eyed Jacks*, Colón would again star opposite alumni of the Actor's Studio in *The Appaloosa* (1966). But the stage remained her forte, and she soon returned to New York. Her next challenge would come as a result of her performance in an English production of *The Oxcart* off-Broadway.

When the production ended, Colón was keen to keep working and loath to wait around for the next offer. An idea had been germinating in her mind: Why not use the leftover sets and costumes to bring theater to impoverished neighborhoods normally denied the luxury of live performances? In 1967, a mobile stage set-up began touring areas that had never been exposed to this kind of theater before. From this beginning, the idea of a permanent organization took root, and the Puerto Rican Traveling Theater group began. "The whole idea of taking theater to the streets started without us having any budget," Colón told the New York *Daily News* in 2003. "All we had was an intense desire and conviction to go to where the people are for the hundreds of thousands who cannot afford Broadway and off-Broadway, so we can let them know that the culture they come from is very rich and very old."

The Puerto Rican Traveling Theater has proven to be a decades-long enterprise. The troupe eventually found a permanent base in a disused firehouse, and Colón worked tirelessly to raise funds and secure sponsorships to keep it alive. Throughout Miriam Colón's ongoing acting career, she has received many awards, such as an Obie award for sustained excellence of performance and a Mujer award from the National Hispana Leadership Institute. But the Puerto Rican Traveling Theater remains a fitting legacy for her indomitable altruism.

Colón may be best known for her portrayal of Mama Montana in 1983's *Scarface*. This still from the movie, with Colón in the center, also features Al Pacino in the title role and Mary Elizabeth Mastrantonio.

OSCAR DE LA RENTA

Entirely unexpectedly, Oscar de la Renta became one of the most recognizable names in fashion design. Originally intending to become a painter, De la Renta turned his artistic skill to a completely different purpose.

Though his original ambition was to paint, a detour in Oscar de la Renta's career path landed him in fashion design. Beginning in Paris, then in New York, the Dominican Republic native found success in building one of the world's foremost designer labels.

SOME PEOPLE DECIDE at an early age what it is that they want to do with their lives. Every decision they make is geared toward that goal, but sometimes on the road to realization, a sudden left turn changes everything. Rarely do most detours pay off as handsomely as the one experienced by this man.

Oscar de la Renta's intent was to become an artist, and though in a sense he succeeded, his art certainly did not take the form that he anticipated. Born in 1932 in Santo Domingo, Dominican Republic, De la Renta was the only son among seven children. His father expected the boy to follow his footsteps into the family insurance business. But even at an early age, Oscar de la Renta had artistic leanings. An uncle on his mother's side was a famous poet, and several members of the family painted, though none professionally. The young boy knew he wanted to make a living with his art, but he also realized that receiving his father's blessing would be a hard sell.

On the other hand, De la Renta's mother encouraged and supported his dreams. Another ally was a Franciscan priest from the church where De la Renta served as altar boy. The religious man proved invaluable to the youth's ambitions, providing encouragement and art materials. By 15, De la Renta was able to convince his father of the seriousness of his intents. The elder De la Renta agreed to send him to the Fine Arts Academy of Santo Domingo, which he attended concurrently with high school. Happy but exhausted, De la Renta was glad for the chance to demonstrate the commitment he had to his goals.

Upon graduation, the most obvious next step would have been to go to Paris, the artist's mecca. But De la Renta's mother had passed away, and the young artist

realized that, with his father's patience running thin, he was better off to play it safe and not overreach himself. Instead of Paris, De la Renta went to the Royal Academy of Arts in Madrid. It was while in Spain that circumstance forced him to change direction. As he cast about for a means of supporting himself and avoiding the humiliation of returning home with no money, a friend helped him get a job doing fashion illustrations for a newspaper.

Fortune further smiled upon De la Renta when, through another friend, he made contact with the great designer, Cristobal Balenciaga. In 1952, Balenciaga took De la Renta on as an illustrator, giving him a priceless education in design in the process. Rising to the rank of assistant, De la Renta relocated to Paris to try his luck with other designers. Along the way, his painting output continued, and he soon realized he had to make a choice. Reluctantly, he gave up the brush. Armed with letters of introduction from contacts he had made along the way, De la Renta headed to New York, bent on a fresh start with Elizabeth Arden.

During his two-and-a-half years there, he developed the idea of a line of ready-to-wear, off-the-rack haute couture designs. Initially receptive to his proposal, Arden then changed her mind, freeing De la Renta to take his multimillion-dollar brainchild elsewhere. In 1965, he took the concept to Jane Derby, Ltd.—a year later, the company signature was changed to Oscar de la Renta.

Driven by a passion for design and bold originality, De la Renta runs a company that today routinely surpasses $500 million a year in sales. Oscar de la Renta designs have won a plethora of awards and have been seen gracing several American first ladies. His fashion empire, now extended to fashion accessories and fragrances, has made Oscar de la Renta a household name.

Oscar de la Renta shows off the 1997 haute couture collection he designed for the French fashion house Balmain.

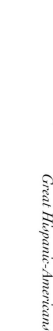

Great Hispanic-Americans

35

JAIME ESCALANTE

In a classic tale of underdogs, math teacher Jaime Escalante inspired his Los Angeles high school students to excel in college-level calculus. When this story went worldwide, Escalante became an educational icon.

IN 1982, EIGHTEEN students from Garfield High School in East Los Angeles took the Advanced Placement Calculus test. Their scores stunned officials monitoring the results—how could a bunch of barrio kids with Hispanic names do so well on a college-level exam? There surely must have been some cheating involved, they thought.

The students' instructor, Jaime Escalante, knew better. When ordered to retake the test, most of the students complied and scored even higher. This time, the Educational Testing Service was forced to reconsider its assessment and take a look at the man responsible for such academic excellence.

Jaime Escalante was born in 1930 in Bolivia. Both his parents taught school in a small Aymara Indian village before moving to La Paz. Escalante would later recall his mother's use of familiar objects to teach him mathematical concepts. For example, an orange depicted a sphere— peeling it showed circumference, while the slices within demonstrated fractions. Young Jaime never forgot the importance of using creativity to reach those you are teaching.

With his keen mind and engaging, if sometimes abrasive, personality, Escalante seemed a sure bet to follow his parents' path into teaching. This he did, winning a position in the physics department at the American Institute in La Paz. His reputation as an effective instructor was quickly established.

By 1963, Escalante and his wife Fabiola were ready to come to America. They arrived in Puerto Rico and eventually made their way to California. Lacking American certification for teaching, he took a succession of low-level jobs and attended night classes to strengthen his U.S. credentials.

In 1974, he was hired to teach mathematics at Garfield High School, a poorly performing school mostly notable for its high drop-out rate. Gangs and drugs were a daily reality—for many students,

the school functioned as a sort of juvenile day-care center. Escalante discovered students barely able to handle basic math skills, much less tackle algebra. Nonetheless, he gamely decided to tackle the challenge before him—bringing calculus to the curriculum—and rolled up his sleeves and went to work. Soon, he was able to find 12 students willing to sign up for an algebra class, and school officials were happy to accommodate him. Determined to bring the students' abilities up, he hoped to tap their potential by unlocking their *ganas*, or desire.

But success came slowly. Cajoling, challenging, and sometimes mocking his students, he appealed to their pride, pointing out that the concept of "zero" was invented by the Mayans, their ancestors. Escalante continually reminded them of how their entire future was at risk without an education and that being intelligent was nothing that should embarrass them.

Much of the story of Escalante's success was told in the 1988 film *Stand and Deliver.* Actor Edward James Olmos captured the spirit of Escalante's methods of expanding the horizons of kids who had been written off by almost everyone. Escalante himself called the film "90 percent truth, 10 percent drama." For all his hard work and impressive results, Escalante has been honored with a number of awards, including a Presidential Medal for Excellence and a spot in the National Teachers Hall of Fame.

Educator Jaime Escalante received national attention from his tremendous success in reaching kids written off by almost everyone. Single-handedly, he transformed his inner-city school into an SAT powerhouse. The students' remarkable scores in advanced mathematics won Escalante an Educator of the Year award in 1983.

BEATRIZ ESCALONA PÉREZ

*From her earliest years, Beatriz Escalona Pérez was drawn to the stage.
This entertainer brought music and laughter to many Hispanics,
but she also did as much behind the curtain as she ever did in front of it.*

Mexican-American comedian Beatriz Escalona Pérez, more commonly known as Noloesca, began her love affair with the theater at a very young age. It remained a life-long passion.

BEATRIZ ESCALONA PÉREZ was fascinated by the theater. As a young girl, she would sell flowers to earn enough money to attend performances. She became a familiar face at theaters in Monterrey, Mexico, and San Antonio, Texas, while growing up, even at times working as an usher or in the box office to be close to the action. While working at Teatro Nacional in San Antonio, Escalona met José Areu, a Cuban entertainer touring with a variety troupe called Los Hermanos Areu. When he asked her to join them in their travel, she gladly agreed.

At 18, Escalona made her debut singing and dancing at Teatro Colón in El Paso. She was an immediate hit and took the stage name Noloesca, almost an anagram of *Escalona*. She married Areu, and the couple had a daughter, Belia, in 1921. During the 1920s, they continued to tour Mexico and the southwestern United States on the vaudeville circuit. Noloesca proved herself a very versatile performer, appearing in everything from burlesque-type dances called *bataclan* to dramas to musical shows featuring traditional Mexican songs. But she became best known for comedy. Through her virtually incessant performing, she created her comic persona of La Chata (which means "button-nose") Noloesca and starred in most of the Areu show's short plays. Her character was silly but sweet, childish yet wise, and audiences couldn't get enough of her.

In 1930, Escalona left her husband and parted company with the Areu troupe. She started her own company, Atracciones Noloesca, which featured a number of other young actresses from San Antonio. For six years, she managed Atracciones Noloesca and acted in its shows, occasionally contracting herself out to perform with other companies. As the Great Depression continued, however, Spanish-language audiences began to diminish, and Atracciones Noloesca had to stop touring. After a second marriage, this time to a man named José

the United States, as well as Cuba and Puerto Rico, that could sustain her company. For roughly the next 15 years, Compañia Mexicana toured, visiting such cities as Chicago, Tampa, San Antonio, and Havana, and established an extended residence in New York City. Throughout it all, Noloesca not only performed on stage, she also took care of the troupe's business matters: finances, contracts, directing, hiring, and training.

In the early 1950s, Noloesca returned again to San Antonio and was married one more time, to San Antonio musician Rubén Escobedo. Although nominally retired, she nevertheless appeared on radio and in live performances and charity benefits. In 1975, she was honored by the Mexican National Association of Actors. She died at the age of 75.

de la Torre, Noloesca returned to her hometown of San Antonio. But she was not finished performing yet, and two years later, she established another company, Beatriz Noloesca "La Chata" Compañia Mexicana, which consisted of herself, her husband, her daughter, and four other performers from San Antonio. If sufficient Spanish-speaking audiences could no longer be found in the Southwest, she decided, she would travel to where they could be. As the Depression neared its end, Noloesca was able to find venues in other parts of

DAVID GLASGOW FARRAGUT

The first person ever given the rank of Admiral of the U.S. Navy, David Glasgow Farragut may be better known as the man who uttered the phrase, "Damn the torpedoes! Full speed ahead!" He served in the Navy for more than 50 years and became a true hero of the Civil War.

David G. Farragut was 60 years old when he received a battle command during the U.S. Civil War. He wasted no time in distinguishing himself through victory on his way to becoming the top-ranking officer in the U.S. Navy.

WHEN GEORGE ANTHONY Farragut left the Spanish island of Minorca in 1776, he never imagined the Farragut name would one day appear in most American history books. He became a decorated officer of the U.S. Navy and fathered a son who would become a national hero.

The elder Farragut retired from the Navy and raised his family in New Orleans. One hot Louisiana day, while Farragut and his six-year-old son James were fishing at Lake Pontchartrain, James spotted an elderly man overcome by the heat. The Farraguts quickly took the ill man, whose name was David Porter, to their home, where he remained for weeks before passing away. Shortly after Porter's death, George Farragut's wife, Elizabeth, also died.

Porter's son, David Porter, Jr., was the senior naval officer in New Orleans. Grateful for how the Farraguts had taken care of his father and aware of George Farragut's new responsibility to raise his

son alone, Commodore Porter offered to adopt young James and give him a naval officer's upbringing. Farragut agreed. Porter asked the secretary of the Navy to make James a midshipman, and to James's amazement, he became an officer in the Navy at the age of nine! James Farragut changed his name to David to honor his adopted father and joined him on his ship, the *Essex*.

Despite his early start, David Farragut remained a midshipman for many years. Even after receiving promotions, Farragut's career remained undistinguished.

At the onset of the U.S. Civil War, Farragut found himself in a somewhat uncomfortable position. Although a Southerner by birth, he made his allegiance to the Union, a loyalty viewed with suspicion by some. The war had been underway for almost two years before he was given a battle command, but at the end of 1861, Farragut was put in charge of the West Gulf Blockading Squadron blockading the Confederate

In this painting by W.H. Overend, Farragut's *Hartford* takes on the CSS *Tennessee* in close quarters at the Battle of Mobile Bay.

coast in the Gulf of Mexico. Soon after, he received orders to sail up the Mississippi River and capture New Orleans.

On February 2, 1862, Farragut boarded his flagship, the *Hartford*, and set out up the river with his fleet. He was a bold leader—in a daring move, he sent his ships right past two Confederate forts that, until then, had sealed the river to Union traffic. Cannons shot at his fleet from all directions, roaring and lighting up the sky, but Farragut could not be stopped. He acquired the nickname of "Old Salamander" for his ability to pass through fire unharmed. Conquering New Orleans was a huge Union victory, and President Abraham Lincoln promoted Farragut to rear admiral, the Navy's highest ranking office.

More battles awaited, such as the capture of Mobile Bay in Alabama, the last Gulf port to be taken by the Union. The waters had been planted with mines, floating gunpowder bombs inside wooden barrels set to explode if struck. During the Civil War, such devices were known as *torpedoes*. As Farragut's fleet sailed toward Mobile Bay, his lead ship struck a torpedo and blew up. As more ships faltered, Farragut, lashed to the top rigging of the *Hartford*, encouraged his sailors by yelling, "Damn the torpedoes! Full speed ahead!" The *Hartford* took the lead, and Mobile Bay was theirs!

Farragut retired a national hero and was made America's first full admiral. His life of service to the U.S. Navy gained the attention it deserved.

JOSÉ FERRER

A great actor of the Broadway stage during the mid-20th century, José Ferrer took his most famous (and Tony Award-winning) role to Hollywood, where he also earned an Academy Award. He became a staple of American stage and screen.

Actor, director, and writer José Ferrer enjoyed an acclaimed Hollywood career throughout the 1950s in a variety of memorable roles. But his talents were perhaps best showcased on the stage, where he concentrated his efforts in later years.

ALTHOUGH IT MAY be contrary to popular belief, Cyrano de Bergerac was a real person. This 17th century poet and warrior was first given literary life by the French author Rostand, who wrote a vivid depiction of the large-nosed but eloquent would-be suitor. To audiences, Cyrano's shadow looms largest over the actor who so brilliantly portrayed him on stage and screen—José Ferrer.

José Vicente Ferrer de Otero y Cintrón was born in Santurce, Puerto Rico, in 1912. His parents, Spaniards both, moved to the United States in 1918. Rafael Ferrer, a prominent attorney, had high hopes for his son when he enrolled him at Princeton University, fully expecting him to join the family business one day. Instead, José Ferrer discovered drama and eschewed the law for a career onstage, much to his father's dismay.

But Ferrer proved a natural, joining future stars Jimmy Stewart and Josh Logan in the Princeton Triangle Club, the school's theatrical outlet. He also found time to put his piano skills to use by forming a dance band.

Graduating in 1933, he immediately found work in summer stock theater. His Broadway debut came in 1935, and within a few years he had his first directing job. Ferrer showed considerable versatility as a performer, simultaneously gaining experience and a good reputation.

His true breakthrough came in 1940's Broadway revival of *Charlie's Aunt*. Playing the lead role, Ferrer's command of comedy seemed to destine him for lighter fare, but three years later, he stunned audiences with a vivid portrayal of the villain Iago in Shakespeare's *Othello*. He starred opposite his first wife, actress Uta Hagen, who played Desdemona.

Staying primarily in the theater, Ferrer did not make his film debut until 1948, when he appeared with Ingrid Bergman

in *Joan of Arc*. His obvious command and presence was recognized from the start, scoring him an Academy Award nomination for Best Supporting Actor.

A second nomination, this time for Best Actor, came two years later for a role that defined his career. That performance was a revival of a part he had played on stage four years earlier, the lead in *Cyrano de Bergerac*. With his exotic looks, rich authoritative voice, and strong but sensitive persona, Ferrer was well suited for the role. Handling comedy and pathos with equal aplomb, he had won a Tony Award for the role on Broadway; in Hollywood he won an Oscar. For many, Ferrer was the embodiment of the chivalrous but self-conscious romantic, attempting to woo the lovely Roxanne on behalf of his friend while secretly desiring her himself.

This triumph was followed by his portrayal of the physically deformed French painter Toulouse-Lautrec in 1952's *Moulin Rouge*. Despite his string of film successes, which also included *The Caine Mutiny* and *Lawrence of Arabia*, Ferrer always had mixed feelings toward the film industry, believing it utilized his talents less effectively than the stage.

Still, Ferrer broadened his artistic palette with a go at film directing, beginning with 1955's *The Shrike*. He also issued a series of recordings with his third wife, pop singer Rosemary Clooney. Their marriage produced five children (sons Miguel and Rafael also became actors). Eventually, he would find his greatest satisfaction splitting his energies between television work and the stage. His last role was opposite Judd Hirsch in a 1992 Broadway production of *Conversations with My Father*, but ill-health forced him to withdraw. He succumbed to cancer in January of that year at the age of 80.

Ferrer *(right)* is shown in 1951's *Cyrano de Bergerac*. His vivid portrayal of the title character on stage and screen won him both a Tony Award and an Academy Award.

PATRICK FLORES

Known as "The Mariachi Bishop," Patrick Flores has spent his life helping others in every way possible. Whether he is singing as he serves breakfast or playing a part in the annual "Kiss a Pig" contest, he is a vital and much-loved part of his Texas community.

THERE ARE FEW people more involved in all aspects of a community than Patricio Fernandez Flores, also known as Archbishop Patrick Flores. As a child, Flores helped his large family make ends meet, and as an adult, he helps others in need.

Born in Ganado, Texas, Flores was the seventh of nine children. His parents were sharecroppers, and most of the family spent time working in the fields and helping out at home. Despite this workload, Flores maintained his education at school. At the age of 20, he graduated with top grades. Already knowing what he wanted to do with his life, he enrolled in St. Mary's seminary in La Porte, and later in Houston. In 1956, he was ordained as a priest.

Wanting to reach out to the parishioners in his area, Flores began to deliver sermons in Spanish. He sometimes even included mariachi music in mass. At the same time, Flores began to get heavily involved in social issues, a passion that continues to this day. He worked hard on Hispanic-American problems and, in the process, became friends with leaders like César Chávez. When Flores became the first Mexican-American Roman Catholic bishop in 1970, Chávez and other activists attended the ceremony.

In 1978, Flores was appointed bishop of El Paso, but he only stayed in that position for a year before becoming archbishop of San Antonio. During his years in the church, he has served as the national chairman of PADRES (*Padres Asociados para los Derechos Religiosos, Educativos, y Sociales*) and as head of the Christian Family Movement. He recorded an album called *The Singing Bishop* for the National Hispanic Scholarship Fund, and to raise funds for the San Antonio Battered Women's Shelter, he hosts an annual breakfast, not only cooking and serving the food but singing while he does it. He even takes part in the "Kiss a Pig" contest, a fundraiser for the American Diabetes Foundation. A very strong supporter of

Archbishop Patrick Flores blesses the crowd at St. Peter's Apostle Catholic Church in Boerne, Texas. The beloved cleric is known for his compassion and ability to speak to people.

refugees, he told *The Georgia Bulletin,* "We are called to share our home, our bread, our water. If people come here because they are needy, we have an obligation to lend them a helping hand."

In 1986, Flores was the only bishop from the United States to participate in a conference in Cuba on relationships between the church and the government. It is little wonder that he has won so many awards, including the American Jewish Committee's Human Relations Award, three honorary doctorates, the Hispanic Heritage Award for Leader-

ship, the Distinguished Churchman Award, and the Medal of Freedom.

In 2000, Flores faced a new challenge. A man desperate to avoid deportation took him hostage for nine hours before releasing him unharmed. It was a fitting end to the situation for the man who once said of legal and illegal immigrants, "Don't be afraid. We have a fear that if we get too close to others, they will contaminate us. No! They will enrich us. Filipino, Vietnamese, Cambodian, German, Irish, each has a beauty. When you experience it, you enrich yourself."

HECTOR P. GARCÍA

Using Hispanic service and sacrifice during World War II as a starting point,
Hector P. García fought anti-Hispanic discrimination in Texas and the United States.
The organization he founded, the American G.I. Forum, continues his work today.

Well into his advanced years, Dr. Hector P. García worked tirelessly to address the concerns of the Hispanic community. In 1984, he was honored for his efforts as the first Mexican-American recipient of the Presidential Medal of Freedom award.

IN 1949, Private Felix Longoria's remains were shipped home to his widow in Three Rivers, Texas. Longoria had been killed in battle four years earlier, and honors accorded a hero seemed certain until the local funeral parlor declined to hold services for him, claiming that "local whites wouldn't like it." Recognizing this significant injustice, Dr. Hector P. García stepped in.

In 1914, García was born in Mexico to a schoolteacher and a college professor. Six of the seven García children became doctors, despite overwhelming odds. Facing the ravages of the Mexican Revolution, the family was forced to leave in 1917.

Things were scarcely better for them in Texas. In addition to violence rivaling that of frontier towns of the Old West, institutionalized discrimination against Mexicans made daily life an endless struggle. Unable to find employment within his trade, the elder García opened a grocery store as a means to support the ambitions he held for his children. At a time when few Mexican-Americans made it past third grade, Hector García graduated from high school as valedictorian.

In 1940, García received his degree from the University of Texas Medical School in Galveston, a school known for admitting only one Mexican-American a year. But before García could fully establish himself in the profession, World War II derailed his plans. García enlisted in the infantry, but due to his medical skills, he was transferred to the Army medical corps, where he earned six battle stars, a Bronze Star, and the rank of major.

Following his hitch in the military, García set up shop in Corpus Christi. Like so many in his community, he grew resentful of the discrimination against Hispanics. Despite the many Hispanics who fought bravely for their country, the war did little to change that. Rather than accept the status quo, Dr. García vowed to champion Hispanic rights.

An endless stream of maimed and wounded veterans kept his services in

Activist García *(at right)* could often be found at the head of a protest march. His American G.I. Forum was particularly concerned about the treatment of Hispanic veterans.

demand. Despite their sacrifice, thousands were being routinely ignored by the Veterans Administration. Witnessing the horrors visited upon these veterans, the doctor was moved to organize the American G.I. Forum (AGIF) in 1948. Though other advocacy groups existed, none specifically addressed the discrimination suffered by Hispanic veterans.

The AGIF slowly built up its membership, but not until the Longoria case did it draw national attention. Recognizing the opportunity the case presented for raising awareness of his cause, Dr. García organized a protest attracting more than a thousand people.

He also shrewdly fired off a letter to first-term Texas Senator Lyndon Johnson, who quickly replied. Although the gov-

ernment had no jurisdiction over funeral parlors, Johnson was able to pull strings to arrange for Private Longoria to be buried with full military honors—in Arlington National Cemetery.

The victory solidified the AGIF's credibility as a political force battling discrimination and also cemented the relationship between the doctor and the senator. As he rose to national prominence, Johnson maintained Dr. García as a close advisor on Hispanic issues, later naming him an ambassador to the United Nations. President Ronald Reagan awarded him the Presidential Medal of Freedom in 1984. Today, Dr. García's image on a $75 U.S. savings bond marks another of the many ways his memory is honored.

ROBERTO C. GOIZUETA

Inspired by a simple ad in the classifieds, Roberto C. Goizueta worked his way through a multinational company until he became one of the most successful CEOs in business history. With some brilliant—and not-so-brilliant—marketing ideas, he made his product a household word.

One of most distinctive marks Roberto C. Goizueta left on the Coca-Cola brand was his slogan "Coke is it!"

WHEN ROBERTO CRISPULO Goizueta and his family traveled to Miami on vacation in 1960, they had already decided to remain there. Defecting from Cuba, they had nothing more than what they carried in their luggage and 100 shares of the company where Goizueta worked in Havana. This was not an easy decision—leaving everything but his wife and children behind was difficult, but it was not as difficult as remaining in Cuba under Fidel Castro's control. "Once you lose everything, what's the worst that's going to happen to you?" Goizueta once asked in an interview with CNN. During a college commencement speech in 1982, he noted, "Material things—your property—can be lost, stolen, or even forcibly confiscated. This happened to me and many of my countrymen some 20 years ago in Cuba. I hope you never experience anything like that, but it has left a lasting impression with me. No one can take away from you what you have stored inside."

Goizueta was born in Havana, Cuba, to Crispulo and Aida Cantera. As part of a prominent sugar plantation, the family had a great deal of money and land. Goizueta attended a Jesuit secondary school in Havana and then Cheshire Academy in Connecticut. After obtaining a degree in chemical engineering from Yale University, he returned to Cuba. Less than a year later, he spotted an ad in the local classifieds. "I came across a want ad in the paper—American company asking for bilingual chemical engineer or chemist," he once recalled. He got the job working for the company—Coca-Cola. Later, he and his family took that trip to Florida.

Fortunately for Goizueta, Coca-Cola had a job for him in Florida, where he was put in charge of Latin-American operations. Four years later, he was promoted to the company headquarters in Atlanta, Georgia. It was a relatively quick climb up the ladder from there, not surprising for someone as determined as Goizueta. "The moment avoid-

the company's motto from "Have a Coke and a smile!" to "Coke is it!" After decades of using the same formula for their soda, Goizueta changed it. Introducing New Coke, he said, was "the boldest single marketing move in the history of the consumer goods business." It was also a fiasco. After many Coca-Cola fans protested the change, Goizueta reintroduced the old formula as Classic Coke. It was a hit once more.

Under his leadership, Coca-Cola's stock increased more than 7,100 percent, an incredible achievement in the business world. When he passed away in 1997 as a result of lung cancer, he was mourned by the business community. James B. Williams, a member of Coca-Cola's board of directors, noted, "Roberto was a man of incomparable wisdom, vision, and compassion. Those qualities benefited not only the company, but the community as well."

Goizueta *(right)* poses with Coca-Cola President M. Douglas Ivester in 1996. Ivester was chosen to succeed Goizueta as the company's CEO and chairperson after Goizueta succumbed to lung cancer the following year.

ing failure becomes your motivation," he has been quoted as saying, "you're down the path of inactivity. You stumble only if you're moving."

Goizucta was madc vicc-chairman of thc company in 1979. The following year, he became president, and in 1981, he was made chairman of the board and CEO. In that position, he created more wealth for his shareholders than any other CEO in history. Goizueta did this by making some incredibly daring—and not always successful—marketing decisions. He felt that Coca-Cola was not keeping up with the changes going on in the world. One of his earliest decisions was to change

ALBERTO GONZALES

From a very large family, this lawyer rose to the position of attorney general of the United States, under longtime friend President George W. Bush. Known as "The Judge," Gonzales became the first Hispanic-American to hold the position of chief law enforcement officer for the country.

As PART OF A FAMILY of ten living in a two-bedroom house in Texas, Alberto Gonzales must have found it impossible to imagine that he would one day be an advisor to the president of the United States. He was born in San Antonio to Mexican parents who had met as migrant workers in a field and struggled to make ends meet. Mother Maria had a sixth-grade education, while father Pablo only made it through second grade. The small Gonzales home did not have hot running water or a telephone. But the couple's determination resulted in children who were tough, strong, and driven.

At Houston's Douglas MacArthur High School, Alberto Gonzales was an athlete and honor student. He wanted to go to college, but he realized the funds would never be there, so upon graduation, he joined the Air Force. "It was considered a victory just to get me graduated because my parents had not graduated from high school," explained Gonzales. Stationed at Fort Yukon in Alaska, he was encouraged by officers to apply to the Air

Force Academy in Colorado Springs. The academy accepted him, and he remained there for two years before transferring to Rice University in Houston. Ironically, this was the same college where he had once worked on weekends, selling sodas at football games.

In 1979, Gonzales left Rice with a degree in political science and headed for Harvard Law School. He paid for law school with a combination of the G.I. Bill, student loans, and scholarships. "My parents didn't pay a dime," he once proudly remarked. He received his law degree in 1982 and was immediately hired by the Houston firm Vinson and Elkins. He worked there for 13 years, eventually becoming their first minority partner.

When Texas Governor George W. Bush met Gonzales, the two quickly became friends. Bush made him Texas's secretary of state, and Gonzales served from 1997 to 1999. Bush then appointed him to the Texas Supreme Court. After Bush headed to the White House in 2000,

Gonzales went with him. He was named White House counsel, and the President often sought his advice. "His sharp intellect and sound judgment have helped shape our policies in the war on terror," Bush has commented.

Gonzales remained in the White House counsel's office until fall 2004, when the newly reelected President nominated him to replace resigning Attorney General John Ashcroft as the nation's top law enforcement officer. Bush spoke highly of his friend and colleague to the press: "He always gives me his frank opinion; he is a calm and steady voice in times of crisis. He has an unwavering principle of respect for the law."

Janet Murguia, president of the National Council of La Raza (NCLR), is another fan. She called the new attorney general a "thoughtful, reasonable public servant and a man of his word." She also said, "During his tenure as White House counsel, he has been one of the most accessible members of the White House staff to NCLR and other Hispanic organizations. We have every expectation that his nomination will be very well received in the Latino community."

In accepting his new appointment, Gonzales said, "Just give me a chance to prove myself. That is a common prayer for those in my community. Mr. President, thank you for that chance. As a former judge, I know well that some government positions require a special level of trust and integrity. The American people expect and deserve a Department of Justice guided by rule of law."

Albert Gonzales has traveled a long way in his career from the fields where his parents met as migrant workers. His legal background has provided him entree to the corridors of power in Texas state government and at the national level as attorney general of the United States.

HENRY BARBOSA GONZÁLEZ

The first Hispanic-American ever elected to the U.S. House of Representatives from Texas, Henry González remained a fighter for the poor throughout his life. He stood for equality and fairness among the races—no matter whom he might upset in the process.

During his tenure as a member of the U.S. House of Representatives, Henry González was an iconic presence for Hispanic-Americans.

FOLLOWING WORLD WAR II, a new group of Hispanic leaders emerged in the United States. They felt that many previous aggressive activists had, through anger and violence, scared away more people than they helped. These new leaders were no less determined, they were just more subtle and quietly persuasive. One such activist was Henry González.

González's father, Leonides, was a mayor and mine owner in Durango, Mexico. When politics heated up there, he and his family came to the United States. González was born in San Antonio, Texas, in 1916. For most of his young life, he worked part-time before and after school to help support his family. During the Depression, he worked up to 75 hours a week for a take-home pay of $11.50. In 1936, González enrolled at the University of Texas but was forced to drop out when he couldn't afford tuition. He eventually returned to college and graduated from St. Mary's University School of Law in 1943.

During World War II, González served in both army and navy intelligence. After the war, he eventually became chief of the county probation office. When he was not allowed to hire an African-American for a full-time staff position, he quit. He remembered not being allowed in the "whites only" pool as a child, and his passion for defending and supporting minorities began.

In 1950, González ran for San Antonio city council and lost by a handful of votes. Three years later, he tried again and won. He served on the council from 1953 to 1956, taking the lead in writing proposals to end segregation in all public facilities. For a short time in 1955, he served as temporary mayor. The following year, González was the first Hispanic-American to be elected to the Texas state senate. He gained some notoriety his second year in office when he and a colleague set the record for the longest filibuster in Texas history. Taking turns, they spoke for 36 hours against ten different segregation bills.

González lost his next election, so he concentrated on supporting the presidential campaign of John F. Kennedy. He won a special election for U.S. Congress in 1961 and held the seat for the next 37 years. As he had in the Texas statehouse, González continued to dedicate himself to eradicating racism. If a bill came up that helped Hispanics but ignored other minorities, González would not support it—as far as he was concerned, this was just another form of racism.

In 1964, González helped to end the *bracero* program, a system that exploited American and Mexican farm workers. He worked to increase the number of Hispanics hired for government positions, establishing the National Association of Latino Elected and Appointed Officials in 1975. As chair of the House Subcommittee on Housing and Community Development, he helped to create legislation that would protect minority individuals facing foreclosure.

During his years on Capitol Hill, González did not shy away from controversial issues, using his office to develop legislation for the savings and loan bailout of the early 1990s and investigating American financial ties to Saddam Hussein and Iraq before that country invaded Kuwait in 1990. At age 78, González received the Profile in Courage award from the John F. Kennedy Library for his work. When he finally retired in 1998, González's son Charlie was elected in his place to represent San Antonio in Congress. Upon González's death in 2000, Charlie González said, "It is a sad day, but I think we need to remember the contributions that my father made. He was so proud to represent this city."

JOSÉ ANGEL GUTIÉRREZ

Often called a "firebrand" because of his political ideas and methods, José Angel Gutiérrez founded La Raza Unida, a political party to focus on Mexican-American interests. Favoring confrontation over accommodation, Gutiérrez tried to reshape Texas and national politics.

THROUGH ORGANIZATIONS SUCH as the American G.I. Forum, the Hispanic community flexed its political muscle after World War II. But by the 1960s, many Mexican-Americans coming of age were becoming disenchanted with the leadership of their parents' generation. Some felt that the tactics of yesterday were quickly becoming obsolete.

Born in Crystal City, Texas, José Angel Gutiérrez grew up in a world where the established social order was undergoing rapid change. By age 18, his political awareness was engaged. Years of neglect by the educational system in Crystal City had come to a head within the Mexican-American community. Feeling taken for granted by the Democratic party controlling state politics, a group of Chicanos, as they called themselves, sought to give Hispanics a more prominent say in their own destiny. It was an issue Gutiérrez would revisit in years to come.

Gutiérrez continued his education, pursuing first a B.A. from Texas A & I University in Kingsville, then an M.A. in political science from St. Mary's University in San Antonio. He would eventually add a law degree and a doctorate to his accomplishments. In 1967, he deepened his commitment to social activism with the formation of the Mexican American Youth Organization (MAYO).

One of MAYO's goals was to educate voters and organize the machinery of local politics. Instead of accepting whatever promises the power structure cared to dish out, MAYO sought political and economic autonomy as well as a retooling of the educational system. Victories included the hiring of more Hispanic faculty and the introduction of a bilingual curriculum.

Gone was the idea of working from within the system—while staying within the law, MAYO cultivated an outlaw image with a penchant for confrontation and the adoption of an Aztec symbol for its logo. To win a war, the organization's leaders believed, one must first become

a warrior. Gutiérrez developed a reputation as a political firebrand, alienating potential allies with his sometimes excessive rhetoric. In attempting to redress old injustices, he would often inflame audiences with over-the-top oratory.

As MAYO's tactics gained traction, the formation of a third party to serve minority interests throughout the Southwest became inevitable. Grassroots organizations throughout California, Colorado, New Mexico, Arizona, and Texas met to form La Raza Unida in 1970. Under Gutiérrez's leadership in Texas, the party won a number of local elections, putting its candidates on city councils and boards of education. Unfortunately, the party experienced internal conflict over goals and strategies. The positive influence of La Raza Unida can be seen in the modern Democratic party organization, which has become more interested in addressing Hispanic concerns than it had been in the past.

Gutiérrez has also authored a pair of books: *A Gringo Manual on How to Handle Mexicans* and the companion volume, *A Chicano Manual on How to Handle Gringos*, using humor and satire to address serious truths about the Mexican-American experience. A couple of decades separate the works, and while it is clear that the struggle continues, Gutiérrez's current views demonstrate the wisdom that comes with perspective. Today he is a practicing lawyer in Dallas and a professor of political science at the University of Texas–Arlington.

La Raza Unida chairman José Angel Gutiérrez presides over the party's first National Convention in El Paso in 1972. As both an activist and a writer, Dr. Gutiérrez fought to bring issues of racial disharmony to the forefront of social awareness.

ANTONIA HERNÁNDEZ

*Inspired by a firsthand view of the needs of Hispanic-Americans, civil rights activist
Antonia Hernández has spent her career speaking out and setting straight
many of the issues that face all minorities today.*

ANTONIA HERNÁNDEZ TODAY fights for issues she once had to cope with herself. Born in Torreon, Mexico, at eight she moved with her family to East Los Angeles. This was not an easy life for her and her six siblings. Her father, Manuel Hernández, worked as a gardener and held odd jobs. Her mother, Nicolasa, also did whatever small jobs she could find while raising her large family. As a child, Antonia Hernández spent time babysitting, selling her mother's homemade tamales, and picking crops.

In elementary school, Hernández struggled. She once told the *Los Angeles Times Magazine*, "The ranchera dress, the long braids and proper Spanish—it was like wearing a bull's eye: 'Direct all teasing here.'" She was subjected to the "sink or swim" philosophy—everything was taught in English, and those who didn't know the language simply had to catch up or fail. It was a tough lesson but one that would later inspire her to fight for bilingual learning materials in all public schools.

Because of her tight family bonds, Hernández went to a local college. She graduated from UCLA in 1971 and a year later received her teaching certificate. She decided to become an attorney and earned a law degree in 1974.

As a lawyer, Hernández gravitated to cases that involved Hispanic rights. She worked as staff attorney for the East Los Angeles Center for Law and Justice and then became the director of the Legal Aid Foundation of Lincoln Heights. In 1978, Hernández was invited to Washington, D.C., to join the staff of the Senate Judiciary Committee. She was the first Latina to serve in such a position. "I had to compete with the best and the brightest to get and keep that job," she once recalled. "It was in the late 1970s, and it was a phenomenal, fascinating experience for a Latina to be able to go to Washington and actually be part of a historic Senate institution. I was in the belly of power and worked with a group of bright, dynamic people who are today at the center of influence, in and out of Washington."

During her time in Washington, Hernández was a coordinator for Senator Ted Kennedy's 1980 presidential campaign. In 1981, she joined the Mexican American Legal Defense and Education Fund (MALDEF), a national legal organization that litigates and promotes civil rights for Latinos. By 1985, she was MALDEF's president, working on important issues such as immigration, education, and voting rights. Her focus and assistance enabled many Hispanics who had never voted before to participate in the electoral process.

Hernández has been the recipient of many honors, including the Hispanic Heritage Awards Foundation Award for Leadership and the League of Women Voters Leadership Award. She lives with her husband, Judge Michael Stern, and their three children near her family in Pasadena, California. In early 2004, she accepted the post of president and CEO of the California Community Foundation, one of Southern California's largest and most active philanthropic organizations. The foundation supports nonprofit groups and public institutions with funds for health and human services, affordable housing, early childhood education, community arts and culture, and other areas of need.

Looking back, Hernández has said, "I'm passionate about civil rights, and 40 years from now I see myself still being passionate about civil rights.... I've never spent a sleepless night wondering if I'm doing the right thing."

Antonia Hernández has used her background in the law primarily to help people. She has held various public service positions throughout her career, the latest being president and CEO of the philanthropic California Community Foundation.

CAROLINA HERRERA

Born into South American wealth and culture, Carolina Herrera paid attention to the subtle lessons from all around her and turned them into a thriving business. Her success shocked her family and the world of fashion, but to Herrera, it was a sure thing right from the beginning.

Carolina Herrera's style is a walking definition of her fashion designs. She was once quoted as saying, "Excess is the biggest mistake that a woman can do.... I like the simplicity. Simplicity and elegance are always very well connected."

MARIA CAROLINA JOSEFINA Pacanins y Niño came from a world of affluence. Her family had long been landowners and government officials in Caracas, Venezuela. Her father, Guillermo Pacanins, was the governor. As the second of four girls, she was taught manners, grace, culture, and style by her mother Maria Cristina. Except for a few rebellious teenage years, the woman who would one day grab the attention of the fashion world was always refined and polished. She was a consistent presence on the International Best Dressed List during the 1970s.

When Carolina was 13, her grandmother took her to her first real fashion show in Paris, which created a memory and a passion that has stayed with her. An elegant and lovely woman, she married Guillermo Behrens Tello when she was 18. After seven years and two daughters, however, the couple divorced in 1965.

As a young girl, Carolina had been in love with the older brother of one of her friends. His name was Reinaldo Herrera, and for her it had been love at first sight—to him, however, she had been simply a young friend of his sister. After her divorce, the two reunited and in 1968, they were married. They also had two daughters—like her mother, Carolina Herrera was the mother of four girls.

In the late 1970s, Herrera began to flirt with the idea of fashion design. Most of her family smiled at her little "whim." Even her husband said, "I was supportive because I thought this would last 15 minutes. If she had said it would last 15 years, I would have asked her, 'Are you out of your mind?'"

At the age of 40, Herrera designed a line of clothes and showed it to her friend, fashion designer Diana Vreeland. Both

Carolina Herrera

Herrera raises her hands in triumph and gratitude at the applause following the successful presentation of her spring 1995 women's wear collection in New York City.

Vreeland and fashion publicist Count Rudi Crespi encouraged Herrera to have a show. They loved her designs—it was time to see if others would too. Herrera displayed her first collection at the Metropolitan Club to resounding success. Her philosophy was simple. "Fashion is change, but certain elements remain constant—sophistication, elegance, and, of course, luxury." Herrera moved to New York and formed Carolina Herrera, Ltd.

Herrera's business expanded rapidly. She moved beyond clothing to manufacture a bridal line, knitwear, watches, handbags, leather goods, cosmetics, scarves, and even fragrances. She made most of Jackie Onassis's clothes for the last 12 years of Onassis's life and designed Caroline Kennedy's wedding dress. Despite the size of her company, Herrera remains its only designer. Her first retail store opened on Madison Avenue in New York in 2000, and she plans to open several more worldwide.

Herrera has survived as a designer where many others have not and is considered as important as Bill Blass and Oscar de la Renta. Her talent, along with her refined elegance, has brought her enormous success and respect. As she so aptly puts it, "I knew that if I made clothes that were real, clothes that women could wear, and clothes that fit, my business would work."

OSCAR HIJUELOS

*With a focus on the experiences of Cubans emigrating to the United States, novelist
Oscar Hijuelos emerged as an original voice in American literature during the 1980s.
A recipient of the Pulitzer Prize for fiction, he has also seen his work adapted to the big screen.*

Oscar Hijuelos's novel *The Mambo Kings Play Songs of Love* became a Pulitzer-Prize winner in 1990.

THE 1992 FILM *The Mambo Kings* caught the public's imagination in a big way. Starring Armand Assante and Antonio Banderas, the film about two Cuban musicians in the late 1940s touched off a mini mambo revival, resulting in chart hits such as Lou Bega's "Mambo #5." Much of this resurgence can be credited to the work of novelist Oscar Hijuelos.

Hijuelos was born in 1951 in New York City to parents from Cuba's Oriente province. In New York's Upper West Side, the Hijuelos parents remained true to their roots, keeping their son distant from the outside world and teaching him only Spanish. When he was three years old, they took him for a visit to their homeland, the only time he would ever set foot on Cuban soil.

Not long after, young Oscar Hijuelos came down with symptoms of a catastrophic illness diagnosed as nephritis, a kidney ailment. Given the seriousness of the malady, doctors placed the boy in a home for terminally ill children, doubt-

ing his recovery. During the next two years, contact with his parents was minimal. This enforced separation profoundly shaped his character, leading to childhood nightmares and feelings of isolation from others.

This introspection manifested itself as a drive to express his thoughts in writing. While Hijuelos was in his teens, his father died, which only deepened his motivation. He received a B.A. from City College of New York in 1975 and signed up a year later for that school's graduate writing program. He was mentored by postmodern novelist Donald Barthelme. Under Barthelme's tutelage, Hijuelos's work found a new confidence and focus.

Finding employment with the company that managed advertising seen in New York's transit system, Hijuelos cranked out a series of short stories. His output did not go unnoticed, and an acquaintance suggested he submit his work to a small independent publisher. The result was *Our House in the Last World*, a novel

about exiled Cubans. Rather than the political approach favored by so many writers addressing Cuba, Hijuelos used a more lyrical, spiritual angle, delving into the inner lives of the displaced.

Though Hijuelos received good reviews, his publisher's limited scope hindered wider distribution. Utilizing his access to advertising, Hijuelos put up a small display ad on buses alongside a much larger ad for best-selling author Danielle Steele. This elevated his status from talented unknown to someone to watch, as the heightened visibility led to his novel being picked up by a larger publisher.

Hijuelos's entry into professional writing was eased with an award of financial support from the National Endowment for the Arts. Freed from having to work a day job, he traveled the world in search of inspiration. The resulting work, *The Mambo Kings Play Songs of Love*, became a bestseller. Acclaim for the novel was capped by a Pulitzer Prize for fiction in 1990. Hijuelos was the first Latino accorded this honor.

Hijuelos's career continues, most recently with the novel *A Simple Habana Melody*. Growing up at a time when elders were respected, Hijuelos developed a fascination for their wisdom and uniqueness. He was inspired to write *A Simple Habana Melody* by a mixture of his roots and the discos of South Beach, Miami. He wanted the beautiful dancers to understand their music and how it came to be. Hijuelos remains highly regarded as an original, authentic voice of Cuban culture.

Novelist Oscar Hijuelos provided a Cuban voice to American literature at the end of the 20th century.

ROLANDO HINOJOSA-SMITH

An author who created a fictional county and characters in the Rio Grande Valley through his writing, Rolando Hinojosa-Smith embraces his bilingual heritage. He was raised to love books, and it shows in every word he puts to paper.

The *Klail City* books use a combination of literary styles including poetry, letters, interviews, and first-person narratives. This particular novel in the series received the 1976 Casa de las Américas award.

IT SHOULD COME AS little surprise that Rolando Hinojosa-Smith's favorite author is William Faulkner. Like that classic writer and his Yoknapatawpha County in Mississippi, Hinojosa-Smith has created Belken County in South Texas. Most of Hinojosa-Smith's writing in his *Klail City Death Trip* series centers on the interaction between Anglos and Mexican-Americans who live in the Rio Grande Valley. Just as his books merge the two cultures, so does the author's real life.

Hinojosa-Smith was born in 1929 to an Anglo mother, Carrie Effie Smith, and a Mexican father, Manuel Guzman Hinojosa, in Mercedes, Texas. He was raised in the two cultures, and the spirit of them permeates his books. Most of these books center around the overlapping communities in Klail City. Although the format of his writings can vary from poems and short stories to letters and interviews, when added together they create a community. The plots are not what holds his stories

together, Hinojosa-Smith has said. Rather, it is the characters of the border area between Mexico and the United States and their perceptions and values that most interest him.

Growing up in a reading family gave Hinojosa-Smith his tremendous passion for books. "I was born into an environment filled with reading and readers," he once explained. "Our parents never forced us to read; we simply saw them enjoy reading so much that we thought every family loved to read as well.... It was my parents' example of reading (alone and to one another) that led us to love books so much. That's not to say we were wealthy, we just took advantage of all the free reading available at the public library and school." He has also credited the regular reading and storytelling activities that took place in his house for the decision he made to pursue the life of a writer.

The books Hinojosa-Smith writes are usually published both in Spanish and

English. Although his first book was not published until 1973, Hinojosa-Smith's first official attempt to be a writer was made when he was still in his teenage years. "My initial motivation to write was winning an honorable mention in a writing contest I entered at age 15," he said. "For a while after that, I lost my way as a writer, unsure of what I wanted to say, but as soon as I started to write about where I was born, the culture I had come from, I found my way back."

Almost 30 years passed between that writing contest and Hinojosa-Smith's first published book. During that time, he served in the Army and fought in the Korean War, taught high school, and worked in school administration. In 1953, he received a B.A. in Mexican and Hispanic literature, and by 1969, he had also earned his master's and doctorate degrees. That first book, entitled *Estampas del Valle y Otras Obras/Sketches of the Valley and Other Works* won the Quinto Sol, a Chicano literature prize. More books soon followed, and many of them have gone on to receive other prestigious awards, such as the Casa de las Américas.

Today, Hinojosa-Smith is a professor in the Department of English at the University of Texas in Austin. He continues to read and write because, as he says, "To write well, you first have to know how to read well, and that's where the mystery ends."

Hinojosa-Smith once said, "I don't know whether you can call what I write part of the 'canon' of American literature yet—only time will determine that—but I do think my work is an interesting part of the vast umbrella of the United States. It's a unique perspective on American life west of the Mississippi."

DOLORES HUERTA

Many would make the mistake of minimizing Dolores Huerta through the years, much to their own detriment. But this formidable woman, instrumental in the formation and continued operation of the United Farm Workers, demonstrated time and again her capacity for speaking up on behalf of the voiceless.

Still active into her 70s, Dolores Huerta is seen here participating in a 1994 march from Delano to Sacramento, California, which was in commemoration of the UFW's first march years earlier.

THOUGH CÉSAR CHÁVEZ largely embodied the group in the public mind, an equally important figure worked just as hard to bring the United Farm Workers union into being. At Chávez's side throughout the years of struggle for justice, Dolores Huerta was also fully dedicated to empowering this marginalized segment of society. As a woman, she would often be overlooked—and underestimated.

Much of her advocacy was directly influenced by her parents, who split up while she was a toddler. Huerta's father, Juan Fernandez, was a miner by trade. Eager to better his lot, he educated himself and became very active in union activities. Her mother, Alicia Chávez, worked long hours in a cannery before remarrying and opening a restaurant/hotel. Chávez was kind to indigent migrant workers in their multicultural California community, whom she often allowed to stay at the hotel for free. Huerta would profit from the examples set by both of her public-minded parents.

Following high school, Dolores Huerta went on to obtain a teaching certificate but found the experience troubling. Facing a class full of children who went hungry and barefoot, she realized that she could help them much more effectively as an activist for change. Her path would parallel that of Chávez, as she too was recruited by Fred Ross to work for the Community Service Organization (CSO) in aid of impoverished families throughout California. Her commitment, assertiveness, and strong sense of fairness won notice, particularly from state assemblyperson Phil Burton, who encouraged Huerta to become a lobbyist. This she did, appearing before lawmakers in Sacramento in support of 15 successful bills directed at redressing wrongs committed against farm workers and migrant families.

By the early 1960s, Huerta and Chávez were working closely together on issues that would lead to the formation of the National Farm Workers Association (NFWA) in 1962. As second only to

Chávez within the organization, Huerta was instrumental in shaping policy. It was she who acted as negotiator for the union, pressing for hard-nosed deals with businesses; it was she who wrote up the union's first contract, ensuring that long-sought rights were among the provisions; and it was she who planned the successful grape boycott that led to the first collective bargaining agreement ever signed with California farm workers.

All of this made her a sort of latter-day Emma Goldman championing the cause of under-represented labor. Being a woman carried with it an additional awareness her male colleagues did not share. Other causes that found her attention included sexism and harassment in the workplace, as well as advocacy for pay equity between the sexes. But like many whose lives are dedicated to public service, Huerta often found herself sacrificing her own interests while serving others. She would find it difficult to be a full-time mother to her 11 children with so many causes demanding her attention.

Still, she managed many great victories. Her talent for drawing together such disparate groups as labor, feminists, students, and environmentalists resulted in powerful coalitions. But the cost of challenging an entrenched establishment sometimes meant personal risk. In 1988, during a peaceful march against government policies, an overzealous police officer in San Francisco beat Huerta with a baton, resulting in six broken ribs and a ruptured spleen. Emergency surgery was necessary to save her life.

Today, Huerta continues to speak out, raising public awareness and advocating political change. As one of the country's great civil rights champions, her good works have made her legendary.

As a lobbyist and organizer, Dolores Huerta saw her efforts to win basic rights for California's marginalized migrant farm worker community pay off with successful strikes staged against grape and lettuce growers by the United Farm Workers union.

LUIS ALFONSO JIMÉNEZ, JR.

Sparked by a passion for art from the age of two, Luis Alfonso Jiménez, Jr.,
turns fiberglass into huge sculptures that reflect our icons and the world around us.
His work can be seen throughout the country in museums, airports, exhibitions, and books.

Many of Luis Jiménez's sculptures can be found in places where people gather. He recognizes that some who might enjoy the work do not have the money to own it, but public art is accessible to all.

WHEN LUIS JIMÉNEZ, JR., WAS only six years old, he joined his father in his workshop to learn how to create neon signs. Luis Jiménez, Sr., designed for and later owned a large-scale neon sign company, and his son was often at his side. In an interview from the Archives of American Art from the Smithsonian Institution, he recalled that time with his father. "My dad was very much old-country in a lot of ways, and he really felt that I should start working when I was very young. When I was six years old—the reason I say six is that I know exactly what we worked on then because it was very important in terms of what I do now.... What made him a good designer was that he was always doing these wacky things.... What he did when I was six years old was that they were doing a neon sign, that is still up, for a dry-cleaning establishment, and he decided that he was going to put a polar bear on it, but it wasn't going to be a flat cut-out polar bear like you usually see on signs; it was going to made out of white concrete. And so I helped him work on that—as much as a six-year-old can, obviously—but I helped pile up white concrete on that polar bear." Those early lessons taught Jiménez the skills of spray-painting and welding, techniques that he would someday use in his own work.

Jiménez was born in El Paso, Texas, and graduated from the University of Texas with a degree in art and architecture in 1964. He has become known for making huge sculptures out of colored fiberglass and epoxy. His work has earned the artist a number of awards and honors: He has received Fellowship Grants from the National Endowment for the Arts, the international La Napoule Art Foundation Residency

Fellowship in France, and the Governor's Award from New Mexico. In 1998, he was given the Distinguished Alumni Award from the University of Texas. His sculpture "Southwest Pieta" has been designated as a National Treasure by the federal government's Save America's Treasures program.

Over the years, Jiménez's work has appeared in hundreds of museums. He is in the collections of the Smithsonian Institution and the Library of Congress in Washington, D.C., the Museum of Modern Art and the Metropolitan Museum in New York, and museums around the world from the United Kingdom, France, and Sweden to China, Singapore, and Indonesia. His large sculptures focus on American icons, showing tribal themes, Native Americans, horses, and coyotes. Jiménez has said that, although much of his work may come from a Chicano context, his audience is all of America. "Vaquero," a

sculpture he created in 1977, was made to remind everyone that cowhands were a Mexican invention, not an American one. "It was the Spaniards who brought the cows and the horses, and it was Mexicans who became the cowboys. It wasn't John Wayne who was the original," he once said.

Peter Bermingham, director and chief curator of the University of Arizona Museum of Art, summed up Jimenéz's art in 1985: "Among the thousands of Hispanic/Chicano artists in this country who are either trying to enter or trying to avoid the mainstream of American contemporary art, I think Luis Jimenéz is perhaps the one who, as a model, serves to demonstrate ways that an artist, specifically with a kind of regional and ethnic pride, can retain that pride at the same time that he develops his art in ways that accommodate a wider sphere of thought."

Jiménez has had strange reactions to some of his artistic subject matter. "'Oh my God,' people told me, 'serious artists don't work with cowboys and Indians and little horses and things.'"

JESÚS ABRAHAM "TATO" LAVIERA

Bringing the Puerto Rican experience in New York into focus, Tato Laveria has, through his poetry and dramas, introduced new insight to this community that straddles the line between natural-born U.S. citizen and immigrant in a new land.

Issues of identity concerning America's Puerto Rican community were artfully expressed within the works of writer Jesús "Tato" Laviera. In his body of poems, essays, and plays, he forged a unique cultural identity for his people.

IN A CITY renowned for its rich cultural blend, New York City's Puerto Rican population stands out. Puerto Ricans are U.S. citizens through the vague designation of "commonwealth," which sets them apart from other immigrant communities. A unique duality straddling both Puerto Rican and American cultures has led to complex identity issues. Addressing these, poet Jesús Abraham "Tato" Laviera coined the term *AmeRicans* to describe the distinction.

Laviera was born in Santurce, Puerto Rico, in 1950. At age ten, he and his family moved to New York, settling in the impoverished Lower East Side. Steeped in environs that were truly diverse, young Tato, as he was called, was surrounded by a variety of ethnicities, particularly African-Americans and those of Caribbean origin. As all groups sought to make their way in achieving the American Dream, questions as to where they fit into the collective nationality were never far from the surface.

Although learning English is compulsory on Laviera's native island, many Puerto Rican immigrants to the United States live their entire lives resisting assimilation for fear that their cultural identity may become lost or diluted. This opposition to the American mainstream tends to exacerbate the tensions experienced within the Puerto Rican community. Conversely, pressures from outside forces, including discrimination, poverty, and crime, serve to promote hostility and mistrust, further alienating this group. Laviera explored these issues with his poetry, beginning with the 1979 collection, *La Carreta Made a U-Turn.*

The title is a reference to René Marqués's play, *La Carreta* (*The Oxcart*), a classic in Puerto Rican literature from the early 1950s. In this work, Marqués takes a rather dim view of those leaving Puerto Rico for the United States, declaring that such actions could only lead to ruin. Laviera took a decidedly opposite view, asserting that one's identity is a state of mind and is not contingent upon one's

geographic location. In melding American self-confidence with Latin ethnic pride, he celebrated a new sensibility with which his people could view themselves.

The first half of *La Carreta Made a U-Turn* addresses the difficulties faced by perceived outsiders in an urban environment. Their alien status is reinforced by the array of harsh realities common to their community: unemployment, severe weather, blighted neighborhoods, gangs, and drug addiction. The remainder of the collection chronicles the troubles society imposes on Latinas, a focus somewhat uncommon for a male Hispanic writer.

Laviera's style deftly blended his two principal languages into a dialect commonly referred to as *Spanglish*, directly mirroring the duality embodied in the American Puerto Rican experience. In addition, he employed rhythms and meters evoking the jazz and salsa music familiar to his community. By doing so, he consciously drew upon the struggles of African-Americans, recognizing that as an oppressed group in this country, they had much in common with Hispanics.

The success of his first published work put Laviera on the path to becoming a full-time writer. His reputation as an original talent was recognized with an invitation to Jimmy Carter's White House in 1980 for a gathering of American poets. His later works have included the poetry collections *Enclave* in 1981 and 1985's *AmeRican* as well as eight plays.

In addition to his skills as a wordsmith, Laviera draws audiences with public readings that are more akin to performance art. These occasions afford him the opportunity to present his work with all the intended inflections, beats, and rhythms, drawing from an array of musical and street influences absorbed during a lifetime attuned to the sounds of his diverse city. These showcases demonstrate his intention that his poems transcend the written page as living, breathing art.

Tato Laviera's 1979 work *La Carreta Made a U-Turn* was widely seen as a response to René Marqués's 1953 play, *La Carreta*. Laviera offered an update of the earlier theme, asserting that one's cultural identity was not dependent upon where one actually resided.

JOSÉ MARTÍ

Considered by some to be Cuba's National Hero, José Martí spoke through his writing to every person who longed for freedom. As he put it, "Like bones to the human body, the axle to the wheel, the wing to the bird, and the air to the wing, so is liberty the essence of life."

José Martí is one of the most revered figures in the history of the Western Hemisphere. Statues of the Cuban revolutionary can be found in New York City, Baltimore, Miami, Tampa, New Orleans, and at several sites in Havana, Cuba.

FEW NAMES ELICIT as much respect as José Martí. In Cuba, statues of him can be found everywhere, streets are named after him, and schoolchildren are taught his writings for years. With nicknames such as "Father of Cuba" and "National Hero," it is clear that this man represents loyalty and liberty to many people. He truly was the symbol of Cuba's struggle for independence.

Born in Havana in 1853, Martí was the firstborn son of Spanish parents and was followed by five sisters. His mother Leonor believed deeply in the power and importance of education, which was something that affected Martí for the rest of his life. In high school in Havana, he showed his rebellious side by working for two underground periodicals. He was also greatly influenced by one of his teachers, Rafael Maria de Mandive, the first person to encourage Martí to express himself through poetry. It would be a lesson Martí took to heart as he became one of Cuba's most important writers and poets.

When Martí was 16 years old, he wrote a note to his friend supporting the upcoming colonial revolution. It was read and combined with his earlier writings for anticolonial papers, and Martí was arrested, sentenced to hard labor in a stone quarry, and then exiled for six years. This ordeal resulted in a leg injury that would haunt him for the rest of his life. Martí, a thin, small man measuring less than 5'6", was always frail, especially after his time on the chain gang.

During his exile, Martí visited Spain, France, Mexico, and Guatemala. It infuriated him that the latter two places had gained their independence while Cuba still had not. He wrote and distributed a pamphlet about the horrors of political imprisonment in Cuba, explaining, "I have lived inside the monster and know its entrails." Martí also went to school during this time, earning a degree in law and philosophy.

In 1877, Martí changed his name and snuck back into Cuba for a month. After

that, he returned to Guatemala to continue teaching. The same year, he married Carmen Zayas Bazan. Together, the couple returned to Cuba when Martí's exile finished the following year. But his time in his homeland was brief. Caught conspiring against the Spanish authorities, he was exiled once more. This time, Martí came to the United States, and from 1881 to 1895, he spent almost all of his time in New York, where he wrote for various Hispanic publications, including *Patria,* a newspaper about Cuba. He also began writing poetry to express his feelings of compassion and his yearning for unity between people.

I CULTIVATE A WHITE ROSE

I cultivate a white rose
In July as in January
For the sincere friend
Who gives me his hand frankly.
And for the cruel person who tears out
The heart with which I live,
I cultivate neither nettles nor thorns:
I cultivate a white rose.

The José Martí Monument, located in Havana's La Plaza de la Revolución, is more than 100 meters tall. It provides the highest point from which to view the city.

Great Hispanic-Americans

José Martí's home in Havana is often the site of commemorations. Martí once described a Cuban as one "who lives from hand to mouth and feels injustice deeply."

In 1892, Martí founded the Cuban Revolutionary Party in the hopes of freeing Cuba from Spain. He attempted to gather enough people to mount a revolution in Cuba, but his effort failed. Nevertheless, he was desperate that no other country, the United States included, would control Cuba. Intending to give another try to sparking a revolution, Martí filled his time with further writing about his fierce desire to see an end to discrimination and racial injustice. He wrote, "We light the oven so that everyone may bake bread in it. If I survive, I will spend my whole life at the oven door seeing that no one is denied bread and, so as to give a lesson in charity, especially those who did not bring flour." He also wrote, "Like stones rolling down hills, fair ideas reach their objectives despite all obstacles and barriers. It may be possible to speed or hinder them, but impossible to stop them."

Martí spent his many years in exile separated from his wife and son, and that saddened him. His collection of poems entitled *Ismaelillo* was dedicated to his son and included the poem "I Dream Awake."

Day and night
I always dream with open eyes
And on top of the foaming waves
Of the wide turbulent sea
And on the rolling
Desert sands,
And merrily riding on the gentle neck
Of a mighty lion,
Monarch of my heart,
I always see a floating child
Who is calling me!

In 1895, Martí's second attempt to return to Cuba to launch a revolution was more successful. But one month after the revolution began, he was killed in a battle at Dos Rios. His followers struggled to reach his body but could not, and he was buried by Spanish soldiers. The fighting continued for another three years, but it was not until the United States joined the struggle that Spain finally withdrew.

José Martí is respected for his writing, his poetry, and his dedication to Cuba. He was not only a revolutionary, he was a guide and mentor to many others. Ramon Eduardo Ruiz, author of *Cuba: The Making of a Revolution*, admired Martí's writings greatly. He wrote, "It would require a composite of Washington, Jefferson and Lincoln, supplemented by the best of Henry James, Emerson and Twain to suggest a comparable figure."

Martí's legacy of words lives on. His collections of poetry were all published in 1913, 18 years after his death. His compassion for other people is apparent in every one of his poems. More than a hundred years after they were written, these works still remind readers of the power of words.

No. 5 from Simple Verses

If you see a hill of foam
It is my poetry that you see:
My poetry is a mountain
And is also a feather fan.

My poems are like a dagger
Sprouting flowers from the hilt;
My poetry is like a fountain
Sprinkling streams of coral water.

My poems are light green
And flaming red;
My poetry is a wounded deer
Looking for the forest's sanctuary.

My poems please the brave;
My poems, short and sincere,
Have the force of steel
Which forges swords.

Located in Havana's Parque Central, this marble statue of Martí provides a regular gathering place for people throughout the city.

JORGE MAS CANOSA

During the 1980s, one man stepped up as the spokesperson for the anti-Castro Cuban-American community. Jorge Mas Canosa kept the issues important to Cuban exiles in south Florida at the forefront of American politics.

IN EARLY 1961, a group of Cuban exiles took part in a CIA-planned attempt to topple Fidel Castro's regime. Once the invasion was launched, some exiles waited offshore for the order to land their troops. But the plan to invade the Bay of Pigs failed, and word never came. One man on that ship vowed that his mission would one day be completed.

Jorge Mas Canosa was born in 1939, the son of a veterinarian who'd served in dictator Fulgencio Batista's army. Growing up, Mas Canosa was a natural leader — opinionated, aggressive, and fearless. He developed a reputation as a firebrand in his teens, getting into a scrape for causing low-level mischief against the Batista government. To keep him out of further trouble, his father sent him to school in North Carolina.

Just weeks after the 1959 revolution, Mas Canosa returned to Cuba to enter law school. Soon after, his participation in student activism against the newly minted Castro government landed him in hot water again. Following a close call with police, Mas Canosa fled for Miami, never to return.

The aftermath of the Bay of Pigs and the Cuban Missile Crisis during the Kennedy administration saw relations between the United States and Cuba enter a period of stable, if extremely chilly, estrangement. The relationship with Cuba was moved to the back burner as the focus of U.S. foreign policy shifted to southeast Asia.

This was a relatively low-key period for Mas Canosa. With the battle seemingly over, he found himself sharing the lot of many displaced Cubans — no job, no prospects, and not much hope of returning to his island home. He got married, began raising a family, and took a succession of low-level jobs as his ambitions slowly took shape. Each of these jobs presented an opportunity for networking and making valuable contacts.

While never fully abandoning his underground political activities, Mas Canosa

anti-Castro rhetoric. Mas Canosa formed the Cuban American National Foundation, which became perhaps the capitol's most powerful foreign-affairs lobbyists outside of Israel.

Jorge Mas Canosa has been credited with single-handedly perpetuating the Cuban embargo. His group has thrown its support behind politicians friendly to its agenda and has worked to defeat any candidate unwise enough to call for normalization of relations with Cuba. Mas Canosa himself was instrumental in getting the U.S taxpayer-funded Radio Martí on the air, filling the Cuban airwaves with anti-Castro editorializing. Mas Canosa came to represent the disenfranchised Cuban community in exile, awaiting the day their homeland may see democracy. Since his death in 1997, the Cuban American National Foundation has continued the work to which Mas Canosa dedicated his life.

Jorge Mas Canosa fled the Castro Revolution of 1959, arriving in Miami with little more than the clothes on his back. Within 20 years, the self-made millionaire had established himself as the voice of Cubans in exile.

allowed business to take center stage. Becoming involved with a struggling Miami telephone contractor, he artfully used his sales skills (and connections) to win a multimillion-dollar contract with Southern Bell. Now the very embodiment of the All-American success story, he had the wherewithal to influence the world of politics. It was in this arena that the legend of Jorge Mas Canosa really began.

By the early 1980s, Mas Canosa found himself, by design and circumstance, the de facto leader of Miami's Cuban exile community. Ronald Reagan's election assured a receptive ear for hard-line

MARIO MOLINA

Studying the effects of chlorofluorocarbons on the earth's ozone layer, Mario Molina is at the forefront of protecting the planet against the dangers of unrestrained pollution. His charitable contributions have promoted science training in developing countries.

IN A LITTLE-USED BATHROOM in his parents' Mexico City home, a young boy used a toy microscope to examine specimens of whatever caught his fancy. The time was the 1950s; although he did not yet know it, Mario Molina would one day discover that the items filling the cabinets surrounding him were toxic.

The Molina family encouraged their son's experiments, buying him toy chemistry kits. Molina's classmates were less impressed, unable to fathom why he chose to spend so much time indoors doing what they considered to be homework. Further enabling him in his pursuits, however, was his aunt, a professional chemist. Under her direction, Molina conducted college-level experiments before he even entered high school.

The hold that science had on Molina came early in life. While many boys find fascination in taking things apart, Molina went beyond that, examining everyday things as thoroughly as he could. His father believed that every good chemist

needed to be fluent in German, so at 11 years old, Molina was sent to a Swiss boarding school. Molina's fascination deepened, but at the same time, another preoccupation vied for his attention—music. While studying science and math, Molina temporarily allowed the violin to compete for his future before it eventually fell by the wayside.

Molina received a degree in chemical engineering from the Universidad Nacional Autonoma de Mexico in 1965. Following postgraduate work in West Germany, he landed at the University of California at Berkeley to pursue his doctorate. There, mentored by Sherwood Rowland, he started on the path that would bring him worldwide notice.

As a postgraduate, Molina began to examine chlorofluorocarbons (CFCs), artificial chemical compounds found in household cleaners and refrigeration coolant. Developed as a safe alternative to ammonia, their use as a propellant had become ubiquitous during the second

half of the 20th century. The unreactive properties of CFCs made the compounds seem safe for everyday use, but no one had investigated what happened to them once released into the atmosphere.

Molina's discoveries were chilling: in the upper atmosphere, ultraviolet radiation from the sun causes chlorine atoms to peel off from CFCs. These reconstituted compounds erode the earth's protective ozone layer, thereby exposing earth to the destructive effects of UV radiation, a known carcinogen. Molina published his findings in 1974, but it would be some time before many people took notice.

Meanwhile, scientists had discovered a hole in the ozone layer over Antarctica.

While such damage can be repaired, it takes time and a suspension of the use of CFCs. With Molina acting as public spokesperson, the seriousness of the problem was heeded, and manufacturers replaced CFCs with more benign agents.

Molina's work has proven key to raising public awareness of the danger of pollutants entering the atmosphere unchecked. In 1995, he received the Nobel Prize in Chemistry for his role in this discovery, sharing the prize with collaborators Sherwood Rowland and Paul J. Crutzen. Molina donated much of his prize money to developing nations in order to help bring the next generation of scientists into the game, furthering the field's contribution to a safer society.

JOSEPH M. MONTOYA

*An able representative of New Mexico in both houses of the U.S. Congress,
Joseph M. Montoya forged a distinguished career in state and national government.*

Beginning in the 1930s, Joseph Montoya became a familiar figure to voters in his home state of New Mexico. On the national stage, he served in the U.S. House of Representatives; in 1964 he won the first of two terms in the U.S. Senate.

IN 1936, A YOUNG LAW STUDENT at Georgetown University considered his options. Though he hadn't yet completed his schooling, he had always known a political career in his native New Mexico was in the cards. Mindful of an open opportunity, he returned home during summer break and campaigned for a state house seat. Despite the improbability of his scheme, he won.

Joe Montoya was no ordinary 21-year-old. The son of a Sandoval County sheriff, he traced his New Mexico roots back to 18th-century Spanish immigrants. He was steeped in deep ambitions and a drive for public service. It is hardly surprising that he would find a way to serve in the New Mexico legislature at the same time he was going through law school.

At 23, Montoya was reelected (becoming the youngest Democratic majority leader in the state's history) and received his LL.B. degree from Georgetown. He maintained his fast-track timetable by winning a state senate seat in 1940 and

then continued his ascent by being named senate majority whip and gaining appointment to chair the Senate Judiciary Committee. He capped the decade with a successful run for lieutenant governor in 1946, serving the maximum two consecutive terms permitted by law.

Lacking any other viable options, Montoya sat out a term before jumping back into politics via a return to his state senate seat. He continued to revisit his past by winning the office of lieutenant governor twice more. Montoya finally reached his goal of a national platform upon the death of U.S. Representative Antonio Fernandez in 1956, winning the special election that year to fill the seat.

In Washington, Montoya established himself as a diligent legislator. Applying years of acquired political skills, he attained a highly coveted seat on the House Appropriations Committee. Notable legislative achievements included sponsorship of numerous wilderness preservation bills and the Vocational

Senator Montoya (*at right*) may have reached the height of his national visibility with a stint on the Senate committee investigating the Watergate scandal in 1973. Here, the committee takes testimony roughly a year before President Richard Nixon resigned from office.

Education Act of 1963, which provided grants to states for job training programs.

In 1962, death once again gave Montoya an opening. Dennis Chavez, who had made history in 1936 as the country's first Hispanic senator, had died suddenly. Though Montoya was widely considered to be Chavez's obvious successor, New Mexico Governor Edwin Mechem thought otherwise. He immediately resigned his own office so that his lieutenant governor could take over and appoint him to fill Chavez's unfinished term. This chicanery, though perfectly legal, made the new Senator Mechem an easy target. Montoya lined up party and public support before the 1964 election and beat Mechem soundly.

Arriving at the culmination of his political ambitions, Montoya quickly set to work and soon made a name for himself as an avid consumer protection watchdog, specializing in issues concerning the meatpacking industry. Many constituencies benefited from his support: He sponsored an education bill for Native Americans, worked to preserve Hispanic culture and heritage, and helped the elderly with efforts to bolster and expand Medicaid and Medicare. As the only Spanish-speaking U.S. senator, Montoya was also frequently sent on international missions as the President's representative.

Despite his record of achievement, a wave of anti-incumbency sentiment infected the electorate in the mid-1970s. Montoya was defeated in his 1976 bid for reelection by former astronaut Harrison Schmitt. Diagnosed with cancer, Montoya died less than two years later.

RITA MORENO

Seldom does such a vast array of talent come packaged in one person, but Rita Moreno's energy could scarcely be contained within one field. Whether as actress, dancer, or singer, this Puerto Rican entertainer achieved honors few others could claim: an Emmy, a Tony, a Grammy, and an Oscar.

Actress Rita Moreno has demonstrated her talent and considerable versatility in nearly every aspect of show business.

RITA MORENO WAS born Rosa Dolores Alverio in 1931 near Puerto Rico's El Yunque rain forest. As independent farmers, her family was hit hard by the Great Depression. When Rosita was just five years old, her mother took her to New York City in search of a better life. She would never see her father and brother again. In an environment rich in stimulation and culture, her budding talent as a dancer quickly became evident.

By seven, she was performing in public. Her Broadway debut came at age 13, opposite Eli Wallach. She became known as Rosita Moreno, taking the last name of her mother's new husband. As an accomplished singer and dancer, Moreno won much attention through her dynamic persona and was signed to a movie contract by MGM while she was still a teenager. Though MGM was renowned for its colorful musicals, the studio seemed at somewhat of a loss in finding a suitable vehicle for the actress. Her first film appearance was on loan to another studio playing a juvenile delinquent in *So Young, So Bad* alongside Anne Francis. This might have daunted a similarly inexperienced ingénue, but Moreno persisted and soon won a small but highly visible role in the 1952 classic *Singin' in the Rain.*

Moreno's exotic looks and trace of an accent limited her casting possibilities, however. Despite her considerable acting ability, she found herself relegated to secondary roles, stereotyped as a Latin or an Indian. This frustrated her to no end, but it eventually payed off when the hit musical *West Side Story* was made into a film in 1961. As Anita, Moreno inherited a character originated by Chita Rivera on Broadway. She ran with the part, holding her own in a role secondary to Natalie Wood's lead. The film was a smash, and Moreno's memorable portrayal was rewarded with an Academy Award in 1962.

Interestingly, instead of cashing in on her newfound Hollywood stardom, Moreno

spent the next several years in a return to her first love, the stage. Triumphs in London and New York solidified her credentials as a performer at the top of her game. In time, she would resume her film career, appearing with such talents as Marlon Brando, Alan Arkin, and Jack Nicholson. Her range and depth as a performer was by now universally recognized. In 1975, she received the stage's top honor, winning a Tony Award for her performance in *The Ritz*.

By the 1970s, Moreno had married Lenny Gordon, a doctor who became her manager, and had given birth to a daughter. Seeking work that was steady and light, the actress joined the cast of a fledgling children's program airing on public television. *The Electric Company* saw her introduced to a whole new generation, with her show-opening cry of "Hey, you guys!" becoming ingrained into the

memories of children across America. The program, which found Moreno working alongside Bill Cosby and an unknown Morgan Freeman, typified her commitment to good works. She won her Grammy Award for an *Electric Company* record album. Her two Emmys came in the late 1970s for guest appearances on *The Muppet Show* and *The Rockford Files*.

Working on *The Electric Company* typified Moreno's altruism, seen more recently in her tireless efforts to help find a cure for osteoporosis. Perhaps for this or for an entire career of fine entertainment Moreno was awarded the Presidential Medal of Freedom in 2004.

Rita Moreno *(center)* is seen as Anita in *West Side Story*, the role for which she won an Academy Award in 1962. Boasting a score by Leonard Bernstein, the film garnered 10 of the 11 Oscars for which it was nominated.

JULIAN NAVA

His family narrowly missed being returned to Mexico during the 1920s, but his remaining in the United States led Julian Nava to a life in public service. From working on the school board to dealing with death threats, he has stood by his principles and worked to inspire other Hispanic-Americans.

Julian Nava has led an inspiring life. Among his achievements is becoming the first Hispanic-American to serve as U.S. ambassador to Mexico.

DURING THE LATE 1920S, thousands of Mexican-American families on welfare were being deported to Mexico. The Nava family lived in the largest barrio in East Los Angeles and was on the list to go. At the last moment, however, young Julian Nava developed a severe case of appendicitis, and his family was allowed to stay so he could receive medical care. Looking back on it, Nava said, "Our life is determined by chance and what we made of the challenge." Nava took up that challenge quite well.

During World War II, 16-year-old Nava lied about his age to join the U.S. Naval Air Corps and spent a year and a half as a machinist mate. After the war ended, he returned to California, where he earned a degree in history from Pomona College. From

there, he went on to earn his master's and doctorate degrees from Harvard. With a specialized degree in Latin-American history, he went to Puerto Rico to teach for two years and then to California State University at Northridge, where he would teach from 1957 through 2001. "With education and hard work, including military service at the end of World War II," recalled Nava, "I was able to take advantage of opportunities that permitted me to see new worlds."

In 1967, Nava ran for public office for the first time, though it would not be the last. He was selected as the first Hispanic to serve on the Los Angeles Board of Education and became president, a position he would hold for 12 years. "Visiting schools across the huge district took a lot of time," he once recalled. "I was busy all week and weekends as well. For 12 years, I was one tired guy."

Nava had little idea what was ahead for him. In 1980, he received a phone call

Ambassador Nava *(left)* meets with Mexican President José López Portillo after presenting the Mexican leader with his diplomatic credentials in 1980.

from the White House—President Jimmy Carter wanted to name the professor the first Hispanic-American ambassador to Mexico. "I was told Carter picked me because I knew Mexico," Nava once explained. "I was bilingual, had an excellent academic record, and had been in public office. I served as ambassador for two years, assessing and compiling reports for the State Department. I traveled all over Mexico, met with professors, university students, labor unions, radical groups, and farmers. It was a position of utmost confidence, and I was very loyal to it."

In 1993, Nava was a pallbearer at the funeral of César Chávez, and he set his sights on becoming the mayor of Los Angeles. Unfortunately, so did many other candidates. With a record 24 office-seekers on the ballot, he lost the election. Not one to be slowed down, Nava instead turned to producing documentaries, lecturing, and publishing books, including an autobiography, *Julian Nava: My Mexican-American Journey*. Retired, Nava nonetheless finds that his life remains full. As he put it, "I feel like my journey has a way to go. I am still running, although a little slower."

CARLOS NORIEGA

It is a long way from Peru to the International Space Station, but astronaut Carlos Noriega has made the journey. A former Marine, he has logged hundreds of hours piloting aircraft and even a few walking in outer space.

IN 2000, THE NATION WATCHED with fascination as Carlos Noriega moved through the space shuttle *Endeavour* with a camera attached to his helmet. Part of mission STS–97, Noriega was there to help assemble the 13-story International Space Station. It was a huge step for someone who, based on a glimpse of Neil Armstrong's photograph, long ago had decided he wanted to be an astronaut. "I saw this man in the white suit," he has

explained. "I dreamed of being an astronaut, but never thought it was attainable for me. I'm proof anything is possible if you're willing to work for it."

Born in Lima, Peru, Noriega spent most of his youth growing up in California. He graduated from the University of Southern California in 1981 with a B.S. in computer science. He had been a member of Navy ROTC at USC, and after college he went to flight school as a commissioned officer in the U.S. Marine Corps. After two years of flying CH–46 Sea Knight helicopters in Hawaii, Noriega was transferred back to California, where he worked as an aviation safety officer and instructor pilot.

In 1988, Noriega was selected to go to Naval Postgraduate School, where he earned two master's degrees: one in computer science and the other in space system operations. At the same time, he worked at the U.S. Space Command in Colorado as commander of the Space Surveillance Center. He became the

United States astronaut Carlos Noriega measures radiation in an experiment aboard the space shuttle *Atlantis* in 1997.

driving force behind the development of several software projects, including upgrades to major space and missile-warning computer systems.

Noriega's life changed dramatically in 1994 when NASA selected him as a potential astronaut. After a year of training, he received the assignment of mission specialist, and in 1997, he flew on a nine-day mission in which the space shuttle *Atlantis* rendezvoused and docked with the Russian space station *Mir*. Noriega helped the crew conduct experiments and transfer supplies and equipment to *Mir*. Three years later, he took an 11-day trip aboard the *Endeavour* to the International Space Station. The helmet camera Noriega wore during this mission was much like those mounted in race cars or inside the helmets of professional football players. The camera allowed viewers on earth to see the incredible things that go on during a shuttle flight.

In October 2002, Noriega helped unveil NASA's new Center for Success in Math and Science at Estrella Mountain Community College. This new center helps students excel in subjects that are needed in high-tech jobs. As Noriega put it, "Inspiring young minds to reach out and make themselves and this country better is what this program is all about."

During his life so far, Noriega has logged more than 2,200 flight hours in a variety of aircraft, as well as 500 hours in space—19 of those in space walks. He has received the Defense Meritorious Service Medal, the Air Medal with Combat Distinguishing Device, the Air Medal/Strike Flight Award, and the Navy Achievement Medal. One day he dreams of logging a few more space hours as a resident of the International Space Station. At the rate he has achieved things so far, it seems likely his dream will come true.

Noriega leads fellow astronauts Marc Garneau and Joe Tanner in an evacuation exercise as part of the training for an 11-day mission on the space shuttle *Endeavour* in 2000.

ANTONIA NOVELLO

Overcoming her own health maladies as a child, Antonia Novello has risen to the top of the medical field to become surgeon general of the United States, conquering obstacles for women and Hispanics along the way.

AS A CHILD growing up in Fajardo, Puerto Rico, young Antonia Novello had a great familiarity with doctors. Born with an intestinal defect, she had to spend every summer in the hospital. Witnessing the suffering around her, the young girl vowed that she would one day help children get through their illnesses the way her doctors helped her.

Antonia Novello was named for her father, who died when she was eight years old. Her mother was an ambitious, motivated schoolteacher who eventually became a principal. She instilled the drive to be an achiever into her young daughter. Novello's peers believed that she received academic privileges from her mother, which only further fueled Novello's determination to demonstrate that her accomplishments were her own. By 15, she had graduated from high school, and she entered college a year later.

The medical condition with which she had suffered for so long was surgically corrected when she was 18. Still, complications dogged Novello for another five years, by which time she'd entered medical school. This experience of overcoming adversity, having gone through a difficult recuperation while in the midst of her studies, convinced her that most limits people experience are illusory.

The effect of such great trials gave her enormous empathy for the suffering of others, that of children in particular. So it was that she chose pediatrics for her medical career path. In 1970, the year she graduated from medical school, she married a Navy flight surgeon and began her residency at the University of Michigan Medical Center.

Her determination to conquer limitations while still carrying on with her life gave her tremendous authority with which to relate to struggling patients. With great compassion, she brought comfort to those she came into contact with, instilling reason for them to believe they could overcome their boundaries. She alternately inspired and challenged patients

Now appearing regularly on Capitol Hill, Novello's impressive credentials and articulation of health issues were noticed. President George H. W. Bush nominated her for surgeon general in 1989, and she became the first woman, and the first Hispanic, to occupy the position.

Given her background, it was no surprise that much of Surgeon General Novello's attention would be focused on children's issues. She pursued the AIDS struggle, appealing for funding as well as further study toward treatment and a cure. But she also took on the tobacco companies that marketed their wares to teens.

After her term as surgeon general ended in 1993, Novello remained active, addressing groups around the country on a variety of children's health issues. She has taken pride in her achievements, providing an example to inspire others, especially girls and Latinas, facing anyone or anything seeking to limit their dreams.

Despite a childhood marked by serious illness, Antonia Novello overcame her setbacks to become the country's first female surgeon general in 1989. Dr. Novello worked tirelessly on behalf of children's health issues and was an advocate for AIDS prevention.

to go beyond conventional expectations. Novello's success drew notice, earning her an Intern of the Year Award from the pediatrics department. It was the first time a woman had won that honor.

By the 1980s, Novello had furthered her medical training, earning a master's degree in public health from Johns Hopkins University. While serving as a pediatrics professor at Georgetown University Hospital, she pursued an interest in AIDS, particularly children afflicted by it. Her subsequent elevation to deputy director of the National Institute of Child Health and Human Development gave her a platform from which to raise public awareness of the issue.

ELLEN OCHOA

Whether journeying in one of America's space shuttles or remaining right here on earth, Ellen Ochoa, the first Hispanic woman astronaut, has provided inspiration to a generation. She's living proof that setting your sights high and working hard to achieve them can pay off.

As NASA's first Hispanic woman astronaut, Ellen Ochoa served as an inspiration to many across the country. To those of less favored backgrounds, she demonstrated what was possible with great determination and a drive to achieve.

As a young girl in Los Angeles, Ellen Ochoa must have looked up at the night sky and dreamed of the possibilities. The time was the 1960s, and even with President John F. Kennedy's bold space program in full swing, the notion of humans walking on the surface of the moon before decade's end must have seemed like pure fantasy.

Still, those spectacular launches of the Mercury and Gemini space programs gave one hope. As Ochoa watched and dreamed, nothing in her background suggested the slightest possibility that she too would one day join the ranks of the country's best and brightest and travel into space. For one thing, higher education appeared to be out of the question. For another, she was Hispanic—not exactly the favored group among government agencies. Lastly, astronauts were drawn from the ranks of the military, mostly men who had proven themselves as test pilots. In that time and place, a young girl like her could be forgiven for assuming she had absolutely no chance.

But Ochoa was no ordinary girl. The middle of five children raised by a single mother, she was not prepared to accept the place in society normally accorded someone of her background. Her mother, Rosanne Ochoa, set an example that shaped the lives of the children, pursuing a college degree while simultaneously working and providing for her family. The power of an education to open doors and raise possibilities was deeply instilled within Ellen Ochoa. A lifelong love of learning took root that would indeed lead her to heights that no one believed possible.

Upon her graduation from high school, Ochoa was offered a full four-year scholarship at Stanford University but turned it down to help her mother raise her younger siblings. Two years later, she entered San Diego University, where she earned a B.S. in physics. Instead of wearing her down, the experience seemed to exhilarate her, for at Stanford, where she pursued her masters and doctorate degrees in electrical engi-

neering, she maintained a perfect grade point average and graduated as valedictorian. (She also found time to win the Student Soloist Award as flutist with the Stanford Symphony Orchestra.)

Following her academic career, Ochoa established herself as a specialist in optics, receiving copatents on three inventions, including a system for noise reduction in visual images. Though falling short of the cut in her 1987 attempt to join NASA's astronaut program, three years later she and 21 others were chosen from more than 2,000 applicants. Years of persistence and hard work had now put her dream on the fast track. Her first space mission came in April 1993.

Ochoa's duties on the space shuttle *Discovery* included operating the shuttle's remote manipulator system (robot arm) to deploy and capture the Spartan satellite, which studied the effects of solar activity on earth's environment. A mis-

sion in 1994 included further studies on the sun's corona. Between flights, Ochoa's responsibilities included duties at the Johnson Space Center in Houston focusing on the International Space Station, an ongoing priority for NASA.

As often as her schedule allows, Ochoa travels the country, speaking to children at schools who now sit where she once did. She tries to impart to these audiences the wonder and awe that are an everyday part of her life's work. She believes that anyone's highest aspirations are possible to achieve through hard work and persistence. Ellen Ochoa considers herself to be living proof of that advice. To the extent that she may reach tomorrow's achievers today, she continually provides inspiration—just as her mother and the 1960s astronauts did for her.

A veteran of three NASA missions throughout the 1990s, Ochoa logged more than 700 flight hours in space aboard shuttles *Discovery* and *Atlantis*. Her duties included operating the Remote Manipulator System in order to release and capture the Spartan satellite.

ANTONIA PANTOJA

Trained as a teacher, Antonia Pantoja was unable to find work in her profession when she moved from Puerto Rico to New York. Instead, she focused on the issue of Puerto Rican rights and ultimately founded ASPIRA, an educational organization far more influential than she could have been as an instructor in a single classroom.

Finding herself in a land that seemed to offer opportunity and discrimination in equal measures, Antonia Pantoja formed ASPIRA, inspiring thousands to dare to dream. For her efforts, President Bill Clinton awarded her the Presidential Medal of Freedom, which she is wearing here.

IN LATE 1940s New York, a recent newcomer grew appalled at the conditions many Puerto Ricans had to endure in the city. Though a trained teacher, she was unable to find work within her profession. Instead, she took a job as a welder. Despite the unlikely circumstance, young Antonia Pantoja vowed to put her considerable drive and skills to use by helping her community assert itself in demanding equal opportunity.

Pantoja was born in San Juan in 1922 to an unwed mother. Despite the oppressive poverty of her situation, she proved to be bright and determined—a natural leader. These qualities were recognized in her community, as wealthy San Juan residents provided financial assistance to send the young girl to the University of Puerto Rico.

In 1942, she received her teaching certificate and set to work in impoverished rural areas. For two years she honed her skills as her interest deepened in raising the standards for children who had little reason to expect much from life. Her work, while satisfying, heightened Pantoja's innate sense of purpose, and she made the decision to establish herself in the United States, where she could find the opportunity to touch so many more lives.

Upon her arrival in New York in 1944, Pantoja became aware of the attitude many held toward Puerto Ricans. Despite her educated background, she encountered what could only be described as racism, both subtle and overt. Store owners would scrutinize her closely while she shopped. Even with her impressive credentials and experience, she could find no employment as a teacher.

Despite her troubles, Pantoja's attention turned to the lot of other Puerto Ricans. Their poverty level was staggering, and the education statistics were equally appalling. Fewer than half of the city's Puerto Ricans could claim an eighth-grade education, much less a high school diploma. It came as no wonder, then, to find so many living below the poverty line.

When her Puerto Rican teaching credentials went mostly ignored in the mainland United States, Pantoja earned a master's degree in social work and set about developing the educational and leadership potential of Puerto Rican youth.

Pantoja recognized that making the voice of this community heard required organization and political clout. But in order to become an effective leader, she had to put her own house in order. Working long, arduous hours at a factory job, she completed her bachelor's degree in sociology from Hunter College. In 1954, she earned a master's degree in social work from Columbia University. She could no longer be declared unqualified for any role she chose to pursue.

Pantoja's first big step as an activist came in 1953 with the formation of the Puerto Rican Association for Community Affairs. This was followed in 1958 by the Puerto Rican Forum, an association that facilitated job training and business development. But all of this merely paved the way for Pantoja's most lasting contribution, the formation of ASPIRA in 1961.

The organization, whose name is Spanish for *aspire,* addressed the high Puerto Rican drop-out rate. The group's leaders identified factors detrimental to completing one's education and emphasized the development of leaders and ethnic pride. Self-esteem was critical; though born U.S. citizens, Puerto Ricans faced bigotry unknown to foreign-born whites.

For this and a lifetime of other good works, Antonia Pantoja received the Presidential Medal of Freedom in 1996. By helping her people help themselves and establish a sense of purpose, she empowered a community to add its voice and contribution to the rich tapestry of American life.

AMÉRICO PAREDES

Mexican-American folk history, in the form of ballads and legends, came alive for Américo Paredes, who spent much of his career collecting and understanding them. His groundbreaking ethnic research foreshadowed academic fields and methods to be explored in years to come.

Américo Paredes pioneered the study of ethnic folk tales and legends. His groundbreaking interpretive methods, such as literary ethnography, ultimately became standard analytical techniques.

AS A YOUNG boy sitting around a campfire, Américo Paredes paid rapt attention as the border "Mexicanos" would take turns singing *corridos*, or folk ballads—stories handed down for generations. A lifetime's fascination with these cultural markers was planted then, and one day Paredes would be instrumental in assuring their everlasting survival.

Américo Paredes was born in the border town of Brownsville, Texas, a perfect spot to absorb the best from each society that straddled the Rio Grande. The family of Paredes's father had lived in the region for more than two centuries. His mother's forebears had arrived from Spain not long before the U.S. Civil War. In 1915, the year of Paredes's birth, South Texas was still feeling the brunt of the violence precipitated by the Mexican Revolution, begun five years earlier. The chaos of the times would leave its mark on the young and impressionable Paredes.

By the time he finished high school, Paredes had decided to pursue a career as a poet and writer of fiction. A high school counselor, however, gave the youth his first taste of overt racism by opining that a Hispanic need not bother with college. Stung by this figurative slap in the face, Paredes added discrimination to the list of social issues he planned to tackle with his writings. Late in his college career, he would pen a scathing novel describing the rampant injustice and oppression indigenous to Texas border towns. *George Washington Gómez* would not see publication for more than 50 years, due in no small part to its visionary outlook that was simply too bold for the times in which it was written.

Paredes found work as a journalist after college, but the experience only made him long for academia. World War II temporarily waylaid his plans—he enlisted in the Army and eventually worked as a political editor for *Stars and Stripes*, the armed forces newspaper. Returning stateside, he enrolled at the University of Texas at Austin, where he received his degree in English and philosophy in 1951.

A master's degree followed, with a doctorate in 1956. Now on the faculty of the university, Paredes had the tools to explore fully the world of folklore of which he had been so enamored as a child.

Pursuing his work with a vengeance, Paredes collected folk legends and *corridos* along the Rio Grande and in northern Mexico. Armed with a deep scholarly dedication as well as cultural familiarity, he was qualified like no one else to catalog the rich legacy of the area's oral traditions. His scholarship also broke ground by extrapolating Texas history from indigenous songs and lore. Paredes's work set a high standard and deeply influenced scholars that followed.

Paredes's first book to reach the public was 1958's widely acclaimed *With His Pistol in His Hand: A Border Ballad and Its Hero,* which detailed the legend of Gregorio Cortez, a Mexican-American ranch hand who had slain a Texas sheriff, becoming a folk hero in the process. Paredes's informed interpretations of the event challenged stereotypes, as he applied literary ethnography to his analysis, an approach that, years later, would become commonplace in literary studies.

Along with his folk research, Paredes pushed to validate Mexican-American studies at the university. By 1970, he was finally successful in breaking institutional resistance against such a program and became its first director. Recognition for his achievements came with numerous awards, including the Charles Frankel Prize for a lifetime devoted to an understanding of the humanities.

Left: **Paredes effectively captured the oral tradition of border Mexicans and helped validate the study of folk tales as a legitimate academic pursuit.** *Above:* **In his 1958 book** *With His Pistol in His Hand: A Border Ballad and Its Hero,* **Paredes explored a real-life incident recounted as a** *corrido.*

TITO PUENTE

Bringing Latin rhythms into American music, percussionist and bandleader Tito Puente made a name for himself that crossed the musical spectrum. In a career spanning the second half of the 20th century, this Puerto Rican musician pioneered the fusion of Latin music and jazz.

Percussionist-bandleader Tito Puente's bold fusing of exotic rhythms with a jazz sensibility created a singular sound enjoyed by millions.

Ernest Puente, Jr., was born in New York in 1923. Called "Ernestito" by nearly everyone, the name was eventually shortened to his more famous moniker. His parents, recent arrivals from Puerto Rico, were not entertainers themselves, but they quickly recognized their son's natural rhythmic ability and capacity for carrying a tune. At seven, he took 25-cent piano lessons at his mother's behest. But Puente was fascinated with percussion and emulating his idol, big band drummer Gene Krupa, so three years later he began drum lessons.

Puente's first entry into show business was performing at clubs and events with his sister, Anna, as a singing-and-dancing duo. His skills were so exceptional that he was honored with awards on four separate occasions. Sadly, a torn tendon in his ankle from a serious bicycle mishap ended any hopes 13-year-old Puente had for dancing professionally.

Despite the setback, however, his obvious charisma and entertainment skills did not lack other outlets—Puente simply shifted the focus of his efforts from dance to percussion. Although his original lessons had been taken on a standard trap set, by this time he had switched to timbales. Not wanting to diminish his odds of musical success, Puente also mastered the saxophone, the vibraphone, and the clarinet, in addition to his first instrument, the piano.

Puente quickly found his services in demand. Underage, the musician was often escorted by his father to weekend dances, where the youth sometimes found it hard to stay awake into the wee hours. But his progress would not be denied, and at 15, Puente left high school to take a job with a Miami dance band specializing in Latin-styled rumbas, waltzes, and tangos.

Puente's informal musical education broadened in every direction. As he honed his musical skills performing with Latin outfits, his keen ear sought out a variety of jazz sounds that were enjoy-

ing their heyday. A big fan of musicians such as Duke Ellington, Count Basie, and Stan Kenton — artists who were continually pushing the boundaries of their genre — Puente allowed their work to influence his own. His fusion of seemingly disparate styles eventually put the young performer on the map.

When he returned to Manhattan from Miami, Puente received job offers from a couple of popular bands: Jose Curbelo and Noro Morales were each playing Latin-based music that incorporated a variety of influences. Moving into the big time, Puente received much musical input as well as a priceless education in the business end of music, knowledge that would serve him in good stead when he led his own band.

Although he had known some level of success, the percussionist's big break

came when he was recruited to replace the drummer in the popular Afro-Cuban outfit headed by Machito (Francisco Raul Gutierrez Grillo). Machito specialized in what could be termed progressive jazz, blending percussive elements from Latin cultures with some of the more experimental aspects of what came to be called bebop. Adding Tito Puente to his line-up brought forth an unheard-of element of entertainment flash.

To begin with, Puente was by nature a compelling and charismatic figure. But his innovations included bringing his set-up, which consisted of timbales, tuned cowbells, and a cymbal, from the back to the front of the stage. He per-

Though highly regarded for his musical innovations, Puente's talents as an entertainer were not to be overlooked. By bringing his kit to the front line, audiences were treated to an up-close display of his fiery pyrotechnics on the timbales.

Puente, shown here in 1999, garnered a great deal of respect throughout his career and became revered by other musicians. He recorded more than 100 albums and won his fifth Grammy Award shortly before his death in 2000.

School of Music. There, he immersed himself in courses teaching composition, theory, and orchestration.

The first years following the war saw Tito Puente's professional reputation grow. His compositions and arrangements were in huge demand by artists including Pupi Campo and former employers Jose Curbelo and Machito. Armed with a world of experience and ambition, he was finally ready to put together his first band. In 1948, a promoter who witnessed a Puente jam session suggested the musicians call themselves the Picadilly Boys, an unlikely sounding name that was actually a play on the word *picadillo,* the name of a Caribbean dish. The nine-piece outfit played a combination of styles veering between Latin and jazz as Puente sought a natural way to combine them.

formed standing, rather than in the traditional sitting style. And, of course, there was his own forceful presence. Audiences lined up to see the teenage percussionist who grimaced, bulged out his eyes, and played dynamic, explosive solos with such style and panache.

Puente was enjoying a great deal of professional success when World War II disrupted his progress. Drafted into the Navy, he ended up serving in a military band led by one of his idols, the renowned Charlie Barnet. Puente's time in the forces served him well. A saxophone-playing pilot taught him the rudiments of arranging, which whetted his appetite for further study. Upon his discharge, he put his G.I. Bill tuition to good use by enrolling at the prestigious Julliard

By the early 1950s, Tito's ensemble, now expanded and renamed the Tito Puente Orchestra, was positioned to ride the wave of Latin music's growing popularity. New York City was at the very center of the latest dance craze sweeping America, the mambo. And at the center of that scene was Tito Puente. Among legions of fans, he became known as the King of the Mambo, or simply El Rey. His reputation reached across barriers of race and class, spreading from the East Coast to Los Angeles. In a competition voted on by the public, Puente beat out Perez

Prado for the title "King of Latin Music," despite the popularity of the latter's "Cherry Pink and Apple Blossom White."

Puente's considerable skills as a musician won him attention from jazz progressives who noted his exciting use of exotic rhythms. But to most fans, he was simply an exceptionally engaging entertainer who put on a fantastic show. For Puente, every musical avenue he explored had one destination: to facilitate dancing. And on this score, the Tito Puente experience was guaranteed to please.

In 1958, he released his biggest-selling album, *Dance Mania*, a collection of tunes that must surely rank among the greatest party records of all time. The set features examples of guaguanco, guaracha, son montuno, and cha cha forms, in addition to mambo. The lion's share of compositions are Puente's own, supported by stellar performances from an array of musicians, including future *Tonight Show* bandleader Doc Severinsen. Overall, the album offers listeners an entry into the world of Tropicana-style nightclub entertainment, then at its pinnacle of 1950s popularity, with unmatched musicianship. *Dance Mania*, which spawned a sequel, remains among Tito's best-loved works. His best-known song is likely "Oye Como Va," which was successful for Puente himself but which was also a huge hit for Santana in 1970.

Tito would go on to record prolifically throughout the ensuing decades. While his touring pace never seemed to slow, he still found time to release a series of albums collaborating with famed salsa singer Celia Cruz. Interestingly, Puente himself hated the term *salsa*, insisting it was something you ate, not something you danced to. These collaborations are some of the bandleader's most popular works, as each artist brought out the best in the other. Puente also worked with a number of other greats, such as Woody Herman and trombonist Buddy Morrow.

By the time he reached his final years, Tito Puente had become firmly established in the American pop culture lexicon. He appeared in Woody Allen's film *Radio Days* in 1987, and he played himself in 1992's *The Mambo Kings*. In addition, he made several memorable guest appearances on television, ranging from *The Cosby Show* to *The Simpsons*. When he passed away in 2000, Puente was mourned as one of entertainment's most beloved figures.

Highly regarded among New York's Puerto Rican community, Tito Puente was the recipient of many honors and awards. He is seen here as one of the marshals of the city's Puerto Rican Day Parade in 1999.

ANTHONY QUINN

In a career that spanned 60 years and more than 150 films, actor Anthony Quinn portrayed characters with a wide variety of ethnic and national origins. In addition to his success as a performer, his talents went beyond the cinema into art and literature.

WHEN ANTHONY QUINN played a man of questionable race in the film *The 25th Hour*, it was an ironic mirror of his own life. For years, he played every nationality from Indian and Hawaiian to Chinese and Arabian. Much of his career was based on playing a variety of ethnic villains. At the Hispanic Heritage Awards in 2000, he joked about it, saying, "I've been an authentic Greek, an authentic Italian, an authentic Iranian.

In 1968's *The Shoes of the Fisherman*, Anthony Quinn played a Russian pope. It was just one of the many ethnicities he played throughout his career.

It's nice to be finally known as an authentic Mexican."

Born Antonio Rudolfo Oaxaca Quinn in Chihuahua, Mexico, he moved with his family to East Los Angeles when he was young. A short time later, his father died, and the boy began working to support his family as everything from preacher, painter, and prizefighter to butcher, cement mixer, and ditchdigger. At the same time, he also developed a talent for art—still a youngster, he won a statewide contest for his sculpture of Abraham Lincoln, and in high school, he received a scholarship to study architecture with Frank Lloyd Wright. Quinn and Wright became friends, and the architect even paid for Quinn to have surgery for a speech impediment.

In 1936, Quinn began a career in film. For the next 15 years, he played parts covering more than 25 ethnicities in twice that many movies. But he finally tired of that and went to Italy. "I didn't mind playing Indians, but a lot of the

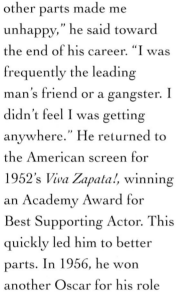

other parts made me unhappy," he said toward the end of his career. "I was frequently the leading man's friend or a gangster. I didn't feel I was getting anywhere." He returned to the American screen for 1952's *Viva Zapata!,* winning an Academy Award for Best Supporting Actor. This quickly led him to better parts. In 1956, he won another Oscar for his role as artist Gauguin in *Lust for Life.* But it was his role as the earthy, zesty lead character in *Zorba the Greek* that most people remember. He reprised this role for a Broadway musical version in 1983.

Some of his roles, however, were less successful. About such movies, he said, "I've a theory about making pictures. Anybody can make beauty out of beauty. But to make beauty out of nothing is a challenge. I do the inferior pictures because of what the parts demand."

Quinn also wrote two autobiographies and said, "I could either lie or tell the truth. I figured the only value in such a book would be to describe my life as I lived it."

His life was an exciting one. He was the father of 13 children—the last one born when Quinn was over 80—and had three wives and at least as many mistresses. One of the 20th century's most honored and talented actors, Quinn continued to act in film until his death in 2001 at the age of 86.

In addition to acting, Quinn sang in the musical version of *Zorba the Greek.* He is seen here in performance at the 1984 Tony Awards. Whether on stage or screen, Zorba is the role for which he is most remembered.

BILL RICHARDSON

A man of many talents, Bill Richardson is one of the most recognizable Hispanic public officials of the early 21st century. His experience ranges from representing the people of New Mexico as governor and in Congress to making national policy in President Bill Clinton's Cabinet.

FEW POLITICIANS HAVE been in the sticky situations Bill Richardson has seen during his public life. With excellent negotiating skills, he has successfully arranged for the release of American prisoners in several countries. It comes as little surprise that he has been nominated for the Nobel Peace Prize in 1995, 1997, 2000, and 2001.

William Blaine Richardson was born in Pasadena, California, but lived in Mexico City until he was 13. That year, his family moved to Massachusetts, where he was an excellent baseball pitcher in high school and was briefly considered a major league prospect. He attended Tufts University, where he received a B.A. in 1970 and an M.A. for International Affairs in 1971.

It wasn't long before Richardson's political life began. From 1973 to 1975, he worked in Washington's congressional relations office. For the next two years he was a staff member for the Senate Foreign Relations Subcommittee on

Capitol Hill. Richardson and his family moved to New Mexico in 1978, where he served a year as the executive director of the New Mexico Democratic Party and then entered the business world as president of the Richardson Trade Group.

In 1982, Richardson ran for Congress in the newly developed Third Congressional District of New Mexico. This district, with a mixture of Anglos, Hispanics, and American Indians, was not an easy one to lead. But this was a challenge Richardson was certainly up to — he was reelected several times, serving from 1983 to 1997. These were busy years for him, as he filled positions on the House Energy and Commerce Committee, the Committee on House Interior and Insular Affairs, the House Select Committee on Aging, and the House Select Committee on Intelligence.

President Bill Clinton tapped Representative Richardson to serve on a number of international delegations. During one such mission to North Korea to discuss

nuclear disarmament, a U.S. Army helicopter strayed into North Korean airspace and was shot down. Richardson was responsible for negotiating the release of the pilot. The following year, Richardson was in Iraq, speaking to Saddam Hussein about the release of two captured Americans. That mission also succeeded, and Richardson carried out similar tasks in Cuba, Sudan, and Bangladesh. He became known as the nation's peacekeeper, able to soothe hostile feelings in angry countries.

Richardson's diplomatic philosophy contained five points: make friends, define the goal, brush off any insults, close the deal, and always show respect. This was tempered by his tenacity and focus. An American Red Cross pilot he once helped said, "He's like a pit bull. . . . (He) grabs hold of your ankle, locks his jaw and you have to give in, or be willing to carry him around on your ankle."

President Clinton asked Richardson to serve as the U.S. ambassador to the United Nations and, later, as secretary of energy. After his service in the Clinton Administration, Richardson returned to New Mexico and, in 2002, was elected governor by the largest margin of any candidate since 1964. Even with all this experience, Richardson seems still to be in the early part of his career. During and after the 2004 presidential election, Richardson's name has often been mentioned in discussions about future presidents or vice presidents. Although he remains New Mexico's popular governor, his political ambitions may one day return him to the national stage.

Elected governor of New Mexico in 2002, Bill Richardson had already served in both the legislative and executive branches of the U.S. government.

HORACIO RIVERO

Horacio Rivero demonstrated bravery and dedication to his country during wartime on several occasions throughout his military career. Born in Puerto Rico, he served the United States valiantly for most of his long life.

HISPANIC-AMERICANS HAVE been part of the national military for decades, but few saw as much action in multiple battles as Admiral Horacio Rivero did. His life was spent helping others, whether on the battlefield or in foreign countries.

Born in Ponce, Puerto Rico, Rivero was appointed to the U.S. Naval Academy in Annapolis, Maryland, in 1926. By 1931, he had graduated with distinction, ranking third in a class of 441. He studied electrical engineering at both the Naval Postgraduate School and the Massachusetts Institute of Technology, obtaining his master's degree in 1940.

It wasn't long before World War II was in full swing, and Rivero spent most of that conflict serving in the South Pacific. In January 1942, he was assigned to help outfit the USS *San Juan,* and his next three years were spent as gunnery officer and executive officer on that ship and others. As part of his duties, Rivero provided artillery cover for the Marines landing at Guadalcanal and helped in the capture of the Marshall Islands, Iwo Jima, and Okinawa.

During his lifetime, Rivero received a total of 13 military decorations, including the Bronze Star and the Legion of Merit. The last was given to him after he helped find a way to rescue the USS *Pittsburgh* when its bow had been ripped off during a typhoon. Amazingly, that ship made it back to port without the loss of a single life.

During the late 1940s and early 1950s, Rivero commanded the USS *William C. Lawe* and the USS *Noble.* After participating in the Korean conflict, Rivero extended his education by attending the National War College, and a year later he was made assistant chief of staff for naval operations. He was quickly promoted to rear admiral, and during the next five years, he juggled impressive jobs, including deputy chief of staff for plans and operations to the Commander in Chief, the U.S. Atlantic Fleet. He also

became a staff member to the Commander in Chief, Western Atlantic Area.

Despite all of the years he had already been involved in war, Rivero found himself on the front lines again in 1962's Cuban Missile Crisis. At the time, he was serving as the commander of amphibious forces in the Atlantic Fleet, and he was right there at the head of the line when President John F. Kennedy sent vessels to the Caribbean. Rivero was part of the plan to calm the situation before it could erupt into another world war.

In 1964, Rivero made history when he was promoted to four-star admiral, becoming the first Puerto Rican and Hispanic-American to rise to the four-star rank in any branch of the military. (This rank had not yet been created when David G. Farragut was the Navy's highest-ranking officer after the Civil

War.) From 1968 to 1972, Rivero served as the Commander of Allied Forces in Southern Europe. In 1972, he was named U.S. ambassador to Spain by President Richard Nixon.

Upon Rivero's death in 2000, Major General William A. Navas, chair of the Veterans' Committee, said, "The passing of Admiral Rivero closes a brilliant chapter of Puerto Rico's military history. Admiral Rivero epitomized the dedication, commitment and loyal service of Puerto Ricans to our nation. He will be missed, his service honored, and his legacy remembered."

Horacio Rivero achieved a military milestone in 1964 when he was promoted to the rank of four-star admiral of the U.S. Navy. The first Hispanic-American to receive a four-star ranking in any branch of the military, Rivero continued to serve in the Navy for eight more years.

MARÍA AMPARO RUIZ DE BURTON

Providing a voice for a little-known era of America's past, María Amparo Ruiz de Burton was the first Hispanic novelist to write in English for an American audience. Her own experiences in California after the Mexican War and the U.S. Civil War provided material for her books.

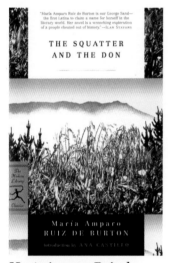

María Amparo Ruiz de Burton's second novel, *The Squatter and the Don*, was originally published in 1885. Heavily influenced by her own legal troubles in maintaining ownership of her land, the book was signed "C. Loyal," a play on the term *cuidadano leal*—"loyal citizen"—a signature used in official letters in Mexico.

THE 1848 TREATY of Guadalupe Hidalgo marked the official end of the Mexican War and ostensibly provided certain guarantees to the *Californios*, Mexican citizens living in the newly acquired U.S. territory. Gold discovered at Sutter's Mill just days after the treaty was signed meant all promises and bets were off. Observing events that followed was someone uniquely positioned to tell the tale.

Her name was María Amparo Ruiz. She was born in 1832 to a well-connected aristocratic family—her grandfather served as governor of Baja, Mexico. When the U.S. war with Mexico came, her world was turned upside down, but life had further twists in store. Once the hostilities ceased, much socializing went on between the occupying forces and *Californios* who accepted the new order.

At one such event, Ruiz met a young American Army officer, Lieutenant Colonel Henry Stanton Burton. An unlikely but undeniable attraction grew between the dashing war hero and the heiress. Once they announced their intention to wed, pressure against the coupling came from both her Catholic and his Protestant church, but their will was stronger than anyone was prepared to defy. Ruiz had charmed the upper echelon of society, and the couple quickly settled into a domesticity that produced two children. They made their home on an estate of more than half a million acres near San Diego. As a result of murky dealings in the property's past, Ruiz de Burton would face much grief years later.

The couple's idyll was shattered by the rumblings of the pending American Civil War. Burton, now a colonel, was ordered east. The Burtons entered easily into the Washington social circle, attending President Abraham Lincoln's first inaugural. Ruiz de Burton was particularly sought after as that rare educated and informed woman not averse to speaking her mind. In fact, she became one of Mary Todd Lincoln's few friends. But toward the end of the con-

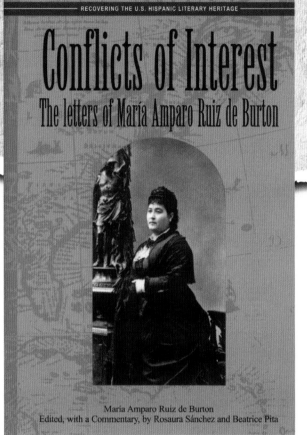

María Amparo Ruiz de Burton
Edited, with a Commentary, by Rosaura Sánchez and Beatrice Pita

flict, Burton contracted malarial fever and was sick for many years. He finally succumbed in 1869.

The young widow returned to California to find herself embroiled in land disputes. As a complicated series of legal battles ensued, Ruiz de Burton set about to keep herself financially solvent. Besieged by squatters attempting to homestead her property, she sought various means of generating income, but it was with writing that her legacy was secured.

She became the first Hispanic novelist to issue works in English directed at Americans. Her first book, published in 1872,

was a scathing satire based on her life on the East Coast titled *Who Would Have Thought It?* In it, she went after what she saw as the hypocrisy of the New England establishment who believed they were fighting a morally superior war to liberate a race of people, yet who remained steeped in their own prejudices about that race.

Her second novel, published in 1885, was *The Squatter and the Don*, a love story used as a vehicle for describing underhanded government policies that favored business interests over moral right. Maria had an eye for detail and little use for the raw injustice inflicted on those not aligned with big money and corrupt politicians.

Ruiz de Burton spent her remaining years fighting the theft of her lands. She died penniless in Chicago while traveling in 1895. But her works would be rediscovered 100 years later, providing an articulate voice for an underrepresented group.

Advantageously positioned to observe history, well-born Mexican María Amparo Ruiz de Burton's life extended through a rich chapter of American history. She aired her views in novel form, as *Who Would Have Thought It?* and *The Squatter and the Don*. Lost to obscurity for more than a century, her works have been republished for a modern audience.

GEORGE SANTAYANA

As the man who originated the phrase, "Those who cannot remember the past are condemned to repeat it," George Santayana harbored dreams of being a great poet. Instead, he has gone down in history as one of the greatest philosophers of the 20th century.

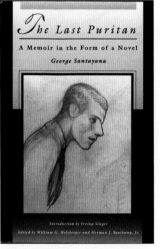

The Last Puritan, George Santayana's only novel, was published in 1935 and became an international bestseller. It told the story of an American youth named Oliver Alden, who does what is right and dutiful to family, school, and friends—becoming, in a way, the last puritan. This path does not lead Alden to happiness or success.

WHEN JORGE AGUSTIN NICOLAS Ruiz de Santayana y Borras entered kindergarten in Boston at the age of nine, he was a victim of constant teasing. At twice the age of his classmates and knowing virtually no English, Jorge presented an easy target. The torment continued throughout elementary school, and it pushed Santayana, a young boy who already tended to be a loner, further into feelings of solitude and isolation. It also helped to create his sense of being a detached observer—the core of his future philosophical writings.

In *The Mind of Santayana*, Richard Butler wrote that Santayana "never lost the sense of being a stranger, always on the outside of everything looking in, always alone." Reflecting on those years, Santayana agreed that the feeling of not fitting in was an integral part of his life. "Detachment leaves you content to be where you are, and what you are," he wrote. "Why should you hanker to be elsewhere or to be someone else? Yet in your physical particularity detachment makes you ideally impartial; and in enlightening your mind it is likely to render your action also more successful and generous."

Santayana was born in Madrid to parents Colonel Agustin Ruiz de Santayana and Josefina Borras y Carbonell. When he was five years old, his mother, stepfather, and half-siblings moved to Boston, while he remained in Spain with his father. Four years later, he joined his mother and family and had to face the experience of kindergarten. Fortunately, he developed a close relationship with his half-sister Susana, who acted as his mentor, teaching him English and anglicizing his name to George.

Despite his late and rather rocky start in elementary school, Santayana did far better in high school. He won academic awards for his poetry and helped publish a school journal. When he entered Harvard in 1882, he became even more social, joining a variety of organizations and academic clubs including the

Philosopher and poet George Santayana rests in the shade on a park bench in Rome, his home for the last years of his life.

Shakespeare Club, the Hasty Pudding Club, and the Philosophy Club. He helped establish *The Harvard Monthly* and was a regular contributor. He also drew more than 50 cartoons for *The Harvard Lampoon.* Even though he maintained his Spanish citizenship throughout his life, he did all of his writing in English. In a response to the question of his culture and nationality, Santayana wrote, "It is as an American writer that I must be counted, if I am counted at all."

In 1886, Santayana graduated from Harvard summa cum laude. He continued his education at both the University of Berlin and Harvard, writing a

Although he seemed cut out for the life of an academic, such an existence never appealed to Santayana. When an inheritance allowed him to retire before age 50, he left Harvard and that world behind forever. Instead, he devoted his time to traveling and writing.

doctoral dissertation on the philosophy of Rudolf Hermann Lotze. After he received his doctorate in 1889, he was offered a teaching position at Harvard. Although he took the job and held it for many years, it was not a situation he particularly enjoyed. "I began to prepare for my retirement from teaching before I had begun to teach," he wrote. While at Harvard, Santayana wrote a great deal of poetry and taught other poets such as T. S. Eliot. He preferred socializing with students rather than faculty and often set up poetry readings.

The early 1890s were a difficult time for Santayana. His father and a close friend both passed away, and his dearest half-sister, Susana, married. Santayana felt more alone and distanced than ever before. He wrote several volumes of poetry at this time, one of which included this poem, "We Needs Must Be Divided in the Tomb":

We needs must be divided in the tomb,
For I would die among the hills of Spain,
And o'er the treeless, melancholy plain
Await the coming of the final gloom.
But thou—O pitiful!—wilt find scant room
Among thy kindred by the northern main,
And fade into the drifting mist again,
The hemlocks' shadow,
    or the pines' perfume.
Let gallants lie beside their ladies' dust
In one cold grave,
    with mortal love inurned;
Let the sea part our ashes, if it must,
The souls fled thence which love
    immortal burned,
For they were wedded without
    bond of lust,
And nothing of our heart to
    earth returned.

None of Santayana's poetry was favorably received by the public or by colleagues. Harvard wanted its professor to focus on philosophy, not poetry. This led to one of the biggest decisions Santayana ever made. In 1901, reconciling himself to the fact that he would never be the brilliant poet he had hoped, he turned his back on verse and dedicated himself to philosophy. He then spent most of his time traveling, teaching, and writing *The Life of Reason*, a five-volume work that received great accolades from scholars and the public. This work changed how the world perceived him. No longer a minor poet, he was now a moral philosopher.

In 1912, Santayana's mother died, leaving him a large enough inheritance that he could finally retire from Harvard and spend the rest of his life in Europe. The next 40 years saw the publication of several books on philosophy to international acclaim. He received the Gold Medal from the Royal Society of Literature in London in 1927 and, two years later, was offered the prestigious Norton Chair of Poetry at his alma mater, Harvard. Santayana refused it, turning instead to writing his first novel, *The Last Puritan: A Memoir in the Form of a Novel*. This was a widely popular book and was even nominated for the Pulitzer Prize, losing to Margaret Mitchell's Southern novel, *Gone With the Wind*.

During the last portion of his life, Santayana lived in Rome. He continued to write books, including a three-part autobiography entitled *Persons and Places*. In an essay published years after his death, he wrote, "I can identify myself heartily with nothing in me except with the flame of spirit itself. Therefore the truest picture of my inmost being would show none of the features of my person, and nothing of the background of my life. It would show only the light of the understanding that burned within me and, as far as it could, consumed and purified all the rest."

Santayana died in 1952 from stomach cancer. He left behind multiple volumes of poetry, as well as many philosophy books that continue to attract praise and attention a half century later. In the first volume of *The Life of Reason*, he wrote, "Progress, far from consisting in change, depends on retentiveness. When change is absolute there remains no being to improve and no direction is set for possible improvement: and when experience is not retained, as among savages, infancy is perpetual. Those who cannot remember the past are condemned to repeat it. In the first stage of life the mind is frivolous and easily distracted; it misses progress by failing in consecutiveness and persistence. This is the condition of children and barbarians, in which instinct has learned nothing from experience."

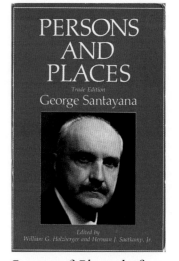

Persons and Places, the first volume in Santayana's three-part autobiography, was published in 1944 while he lived at a nursing home run by the Blue Sisters in Rome. He found spiritual comfort there, even though he often described himself as "divorced" from any religious faith.

ARTHUR ALFONSO SCHOMBURG

Sometimes referred to as "The Sherlock Holmes of Negro History," bibliophile Arthur Schomburg made it his life's goal to preserve African-American heritage for generations to come. He merged races, considering himself a true "afroborinqueño," or a black Puerto Rican.

Arthur Schomburg's Pan-African collection was a touchstone for African cultural identity. It can still be seen at the New York Public Library's Schomburg Center for Research in Black Culture.

ALTHOUGH MANY PUBLIC school teachers hope they will be an inspiration to their students, Arthur Alfonso Schomburg's fifth grade teacher in Puerto Rico could never have realized how her words would affect him. When she informed her class that the black people had no heroes, no history, and no worthy heritage, Schomburg was stunned, shocked, and disbelieving. How could an entire people not have an important culture and role models? From that moment on, it became his dream to prove his teacher wrong.

Schomburg was born in Puerto Rico in 1874 to mother Mary Joseph, who came from the Virgin Islands, and father Carlos Federico, a German merchant. Schomburg's father played only a small part in his son's life. Mary Joseph Schomburg wanted her son to have an education, but that was not easy to find in Puerto Rico in the late 1800s. When he turned 17, Schomburg left the island and went to New York City, where he had a succession of temporary jobs, including porter, printer, and hotel bellhop, as he went to high school. Those years showed him the tremendous amount of racism against both the black and Hispanic cultures in the United States. Schomburg would dedicate the rest of his life to eradicating that racism.

Throughout his life, Schomburg joined and/or founded many different organizations, such as the Negro Society for Historical Research and *Las Dos Antillas*. The name of the latter organization means "the two islands," which referred to the group's support of Cuban and Puerto Rican independence from Spain. Schomburg's main focus, however, was on the slow but deliberate collection of Pan-African literature and art from the "African diaspora." He began by gathering journal entries, letters, essays, books, artwork, and pamphlets created by blacks and went on to correspond regularly with civil rights leaders such as W.E.B. DuBois, Booker T. Washington, and James Weldon Johnson. He once summed up his philosophy as an archivist:

"The American Negro must rebuild his past in order to make his future."

By 1911, Schomburg's collection was taking over his house, and scholars were stopping by daily to look through his vast store of materials. It was not long before he began receiving offers to purchase the "Schomburg Collection of Negro Literature and History." In 1925, he went to Europe to locate more literature and artwork for his collection. This concentration of materials provided one focus for the Harlem Renaissance, an African-American literary and social movement that flourished in the 1920s. Finally, in 1926, Schomburg sold his collection for $10,000 to the New York Public Library. At that time, he had 2,932 books, 1,124 pamphlets, and much more. Everything was moved to Harlem and, in 1934, was opened to the public. Schomburg was the curator of the collection until his death in 1938.

At a memorial service for Schomburg, Charles Spurgeon Johnson called the collection "a visible monument to the life's work of Arthur Schomburg." He went on to say, "It stands for itself, quietly and solidly for all time, a rich and inexhaustible treasure store for scholars and laymen alike, the materialization of the foresight, industry, and scholarship" of the dedicated bibliophile.

Looking back on Schomburg's life, Richard Perez, director of the New York-based Community Service Society of New York, said, "Puerto Ricans are a multiracial people...and as a multiracial people, it was difficult for us to establish our identity in a country that defines racial identity only as black and white. Schomburg's research in that direction had made it a little easier, and was a contribution that we have been able to build on."

Schomburg *(standing, second from right)* **attends the unveiling of a bust of 19th-century African-American actor Ira Aldridge as Othello. This bust is currently part of the collection of the Schomburg Center.**

MARTIN SHEEN

An actor practicing his craft and an activist for peace and justice, Martin Sheen is familiar from his many roles—often as a political leader—on television and in movies. He has used his high profile to take stands on a number of social issues.

Born Ramón Estévez, actor Martin Sheen has portrayed political leaders, both historic and fictional. He may be best known today for his portrayal of President Josiah Bartlet in television's *The West Wing*.

MARTIN SHEEN HAS made a career of playing authority figures. Whether as attorney general Robert Kennedy or as Confederate General Robert E. Lee, Sheen seems to possess an effortless gravitas.

Sheen's unlikely rise to stardom began in Dayton, Ohio. The seventh of ten children, he was born in 1940 as Ramón Estévez. His parents were recent U.S. citizens, his mother arriving from Ireland and his father from Spain via Cuba. Steeped in Old World Catholicism, their ties to the church would become essential to the family's survival after Mrs. Estévez died when Ramón was young.

Somewhere along the line, Ramón Estévez caught the acting bug. Though his father had worked hard to provide for his children's education, the youth had

other plans. Knowing his father's disapproval of his acting aspirations, Estévez purposely flunked his college entrance exams. Then, abetted by a friendly priest who loaned him the necessary funds, he bought a bus ticket to New York.

While seeking jobs through agents over the phone, Estévez discovered that his Hispanic name won him mostly ethnic roles. He therefore assumed the professional name of Martin Sheen: "Martin" after a CBS casting director who had championed him, and "Sheen" after famous religious broadcaster Bishop Fulton Sheen. But Martin Sheen is a stage name—he has never had his name legally changed. "I'm very proud of my Hispanic heritage," he has said. "I never changed my name. I never will. In the context of the business, I had to adapt to a way of nonconfrontation 40 years ago, so I invented myself. I invented Martin Sheen. Within my heart I'm still Ramón."

Sheen found steady work in television. This provided regular income as he mar-

ried wife Janet in December 1961 and started a family, beginning with son Emilio in 1962. Eventually, all four of Sheen's children would enter acting, but only son Charlie (born Carlos) would adopt his father's stage name.

With *Badlands* in 1973, Martin Sheen achieved widespread notice on the silver screen. It is ironic that the man whose career would be defined by portrayals of presidents and politicians first reached film audiences as a hard-boiled criminal.

As Captain Willard in Francis Ford Coppola's *Apocalypse Now*, Sheen gave a stunning performance—the actor notably held his own against the legendary Marlon Brando. Sheen, 39, suffered a heart attack during filming. He later called this grueling filmmaking experience in the jungles of the Philippines life changing and said it led to his eventual swearing off of bad habits and redoubling his faith.

Sheen's values are often seen in the form of political activism. Aligning himself with various social justice causes through

the years, such as fighting nuclear proliferation and militarism, he has often allowed himself to be arrested to make a point. His first arrest came in 1986 during a protest against the U.S. Strategic Defense Initiative, more commonly known as Star Wars. "That arrest was one of the happiest moments of my life and, equally, one of the scariest," he later said. While detractors may claim that political posturing is good for a career, Sheen argues the opposite, that his high-profile beliefs have cost him work.

Still, something about his persona has made him ideally suited to portraying leaders. Sheen landed the lead role in the highly acclaimed television series *The West Wing* in 1999. For someone of Sheen's background and beliefs, the role is a perfect fit, embodying a culmination of the American dream.

Never one to shy away from controversy, Sheen has made getting arrested at political demonstrations something of a second career. Here he is seen at a protest outside California's Vandenberg Air Force Base in October 2000.

REIES LÓPEZ TIJERINA

Called "King Tiger," militant activist Reies López Tijerina brought hope and pride to some Hispanics and, at the same time, shocked and frightened others. He fought to return land to its original owners, which was a struggle that affected Mexican-Americans across the country.

URING THE 1960s and 1970s, militant leaders began to emerge from the Hispanic community. These people disagreed with the nonviolent ways of César Chávez, feeling they were ineffective. Instead, the new activists focused on fighting for change, no matter the cost. One of the most intensely aggressive leaders was Reies López Tijerina.

Born to migrant workers near Falls City, Texas, Tijerina's early life was spent working in the fields and moving from place to place. As an adult he learned about the 1848 Treaty of Guadalupe Hidalgo, which had been signed by Mexico and the United States after a bloody war between the countries. The treaty ceded large amounts of Mexican territory to the United States but was supposed to protect the property rights of Mexicans living in that territory. Needless to say, these intentions were not vigorously defended, and the United States government quickly began to expand into what had been Mexican land. Tijerina wanted to return those millions of acres to what he saw as their rightful owners.

In 1963, Tijerina established the *Alianza Federal de Mercedes* (Federal Alliance of Land Grants). Over time, Alianza membership came to number in the thousands. But despite their passion, they could not get any government or courts to listen to their argument. Finally, Tijerina and 350 - others took over part of New Mexico's Kit Carson National Forest in 1966, renaming it the Republic of San Joaquin. When police and park rangers attempted to remove the protesters, Alianza made citizen arrests of them for trespassing in the new country. Federal charges were filed against Tijerina.

Later, Tijerina and an armed group attacked the courthouse in Tierra Amarilla, New Mexico. They planned to make a citizen's arrest of the district attorney but were unable to find him. During the incident, the group took a reporter and deputy sheriff hostage, and a police officer was shot and wounded.

When the attackers escaped, a huge search followed—tanks, helicopters, and the National Guard combed the territory. Tijerina eventually agreed to give himself up, but while out on bail, he tried once again to take over Kit Carson National Forest. This time, he was charged with pointing a gun at officers who had reportedly threatened his wife.

In a letter written from jail, Tijerina argued: "What is my real crime? As I and the poor people see it, especially the Indo-Hispanos, *my only crime is upholding our rights as protected by the Treaty of Guadalupe Hidalgo*, which ended the so-called Mexican-American War of 1846–1848." Tijerina represented himself in court, where he was found not guilty. In a separate trial concerning the first Kit Carson National Park incident, he was not as successful. He was found guilty verdict and received a prison sentence.

After his release from prison, Tijerina was prohibited from again becoming involved with Alianza and kept a much lower public profile. In 1999, the University of New Mexico honored him for contributing his papers to its library. Civil rights activist and publisher Jose Armas has said Tijerina's effect on Hispanics was immense. "The impact of what he did is felt by 99 percent of Latinos, even though they may not know it came from him. . . . He created pride. He instilled hope. He made an impact on society in general," Armas said. But he also noted that the full extent of Tijerina's influence goes still further. "Some of the most significant contributions he made were to educate us about our beginnings. He talked about elements of history that had seldom been heard before. He said, 'If you don't know history, you can't have a future.'"

During the 1960s, Reies López Tijerina was the leading advocate of land reform in the Southwest. In 1968, he was invited by Dr. Martin Luther King, Jr., to join the civil rights leader's Poor People's Campaign (PPC). Following King's assassination, Tijerina took part in the Poor People's March on Washington. Here he addresses a 1968 PPC rally in Kansas City, Missouri.

JOSEPH A. UNANUE

Entrepreneur Joseph A. Unanue's story is a reminder to all minorities that success can come through their heritage. From a company geared toward the tastes of immigrants to a label found in most grocery stores, this story is an example of persistence.

Joseph Unanue's business plan was to market to Hispanics entering the United States with familiar products from their home countries. Goya Foods used colorful advertising such as this to meet that goal.

WHEN PRUDENCIO UNANUE first attempted to import olives and canned sardines from Spain to New York in the 1920s, he could not have imagined that his faltering business would one day be worth $750 million. When the Spanish Civil War interrupted exports from that country in 1936, Unanue and his wife Carolina established their own company to manufacture and market the products, which became Goya Foods. The Unanues wanted to provide immigrants with the flavors they had left behind when coming to the United States, and it was an idea that continued to grow. Today, Goya Foods is the United States' largest Hispanic-owned food business.

The Unanue family had four sons, including Joseph, born in New York. After a brief time serving in the Army during World War II, Joseph Unanue earned a degree in engineering from the Catholic University of America in Washington, D.C. But instead of becoming an engineer, he joined his

brothers Frank, Anthony, and Charles in the family business. When Prudencio passed away in 1976, Joseph became the company's president.

Several important business decisions helped Goya Foods become a mega-business. First, in a move to produce foods that appealed to Hispanics of all backgrounds, products such as cactus paddles (nopalitos) from Mexico and beef tripe stew (mondongo) from the Caribbean were added to the company line. Second, Joseph Unanue was determined to reach out beyond the typical small Mexican markets in which his products were sold and into mainstream stores where non-Hispanics could also enjoy the ethnic foods. "I think that entrepreneurs of ethnic backgrounds need to try to meld better into the rest of the country," he once wrote. "It's important to help yourself and your heritage, but it's equally important to help the country, in the business sense, as well." Goya Food products began to expand into the Safeway, Albertson's, and

Jews. He was twice given the National Hispanic Achievement Award.

Throughout its history, the Goya Foods Corporation has been firm in its emphasis on keeping everything in the family. The entire company is owned by the descendants of Prudencio and Carolina Unanue, down to second, third, and fourth generations. In 2004, the board of directors restructured the leadership of Goya Foods, and Joseph Unanue left his post as president and CEO of the company. Goya's sales had grown to almost 100 times what they had been in 1976 when Unanue assumed the top position in the company. At 78, Joseph Unanue could look back at his tenure with an enormous amount of pride in his many accomplishments.

Wal-Mart chains across the country. "Starting with a Safeway up in Harlem, we began to win them over," explained Unanue. "Then came A&P. But it was because of our heritage, our ethnicity, that we got the advantage."

Over the years, Unanue became a civic leader in both the mainland United States and Puerto Rico. He has been the recipient of numerous awards, including the Ellis Island Medal of Honor and the Man of the Year award from the National Conference of Christians and

Joseph Unanue expanded the family business from a specialized ethnic food company to become a staple of mainstream grocery stores. Perhaps most surprising is that he accomplished this feat without minimizing the Hispanic identity of Goya Foods.

LUIS VALDEZ

As activists César Chávez and Dolores Huerta crusaded on behalf of migrant farm workers in the mid-1960s, an aspiring actor and playwright became drawn to their cause as a sort of homecoming. Utilizing his abilities, he began staging plays as a way to contribute and draw attention to the plight of the farm workers. Not long before, he'd been one of them.

Playwright and director Luis Valdez first established himself with El Teatro Campesino, the cultural offshoot of César Chávez's farm workers' labor union. By staging one-act plays depicting the migrant worker's struggle, Valdez helped draw attention to the cause while rallying the troops.

HIS NAME WAS Luis Valdez, and he was born into a family of migrant farm workers, the second of ten children, in Delano, California. Such a circumstance meant he was constantly being uprooted and his education disrupted. But it was in a classroom setting that the first spark of what would become his life's pursuit was lit.

When he was six, Valdez watched as a teacher used a paper bag to create a papier-mâché mask for a school play. To call the experience life changing would be little exaggeration, for it kindled within him an interest in theater that would blossom in years to come. Despite the odds against a child of itinerant farm workers making something of himself, Francesco and Armeda Valdez were determined to keep their children from following them into the field—literally. Education, they knew, was the key to escaping certain poverty. They would direct all of their labors to ensuring that their kids would realize the American dream.

At 18, Luis won a scholarship to San Jose State College, as his brother had shortly before. No one in their family had ever gotten so far in their education, and Luis was deeply aware of the opportunity he had been given. To honor his parents' wishes, he initially declared as a math and physics major, but the draw of theater was too strong. Within a year, he gave in to his nature and switched to English.

He had already been hard at work, honing his skills in dramatics. A one-act play he'd written, *The Thief,* had won an award in 1961. Before Luis completed his bachelor's degree, his full-length drama, *The Shrunken Head of Pancho Villa,* would be produced by the school's theater department. It drew praise from no less an authority than writer William Saroyan.

Following his graduation in 1964, Valdez began working with the San Francisco Mime Troupe, where he learned the fundamentals of agitprop theater, a form of theatrics meant to espouse a particular viewpoint and provoke response.

Agitprop tactics would become extremely useful when Valdez decided to return to Delano, where the burgeoning farm worker's rights movement was beginning to take shape.

In 1965, he joined the National Farm Workers Association and began laying the groundwork for El Teatro Campesino, which would serve as a de facto cultural branch of César Chávez's organization. As artistic director and playwright-in-residence, Valdez set up a troupe that toured the workers' camps, performing improvisational morality plays on flatbed trucks. Though many farm workers could neither read nor write, they were able to recognize their lives as presented onstage. Valdez's one-act dramas had a galvanizing effect on audiences, inspiring the troops while bringing public attention (and financial support) to their cause.

El Teatro Campesino proved quite successful in achieving its goals of shaping public opinion. The effectiveness of

theater was not lost on Valdez, who soon had larger ideas. Feeling that the reach of a theatrical group tied to the union was limited and suffering the inevitable limitations union control placed upon his art, Valdez left the organization in 1967 to promote El Teatro Campesino as a self-standing vehicle for politically driven Chicano theater.

His group toured the country for its first year of independence, broadening its scope beyond migrant concerns with presentations that drew upon traditional Mexican art forms. Ballads, dance, and religious as well as comedic elements were all woven together to form a uniquely Hispanic experience. By the time the company was ready to settle in its home in Fresno, it had received an

Valdez made his mainstream Hollywood directorial debut with an adaptation of his own play, *Zoot Suit,* in 1982. Though Valdez is often associated with overtly political works, the film *La Bamba* demonstrated his ability to churn out traditional Hollywood entertainment with the best of them.

Valdez *(right)* shows César Chávez the sights while standing in front of New York's Winter Garden Theater during the 1979 Broadway run of *Zoot Suit.*

post at the University of California at Berkeley. But the lure of commercial enterprise beckoned, and in 1977, he took his first Hollywood job. Both Luis Valdez and his brother Daniel appeared in the Richard Pryor film, *Which Way Is Up?* Although the film was not a hit, it gave Valdez an industry foothold that would pay off down the road.

A Broadway production resulted in an honorarium bestowed by the Rockefeller Foundation, naming Valdez Playwright-in-Residence. The award gave him the wherewithal to write a play based on true events that followed an unsolved Los Angeles murder during the 1940s. *Zoot Suit* became the means through which Valdez was able to illustrate the ignorance, prejudice, and violence inflicted upon Chicano youth at the hands of the police, the courts, and thuggish bands of carousing white sailors and soldiers on leave during World War II. Once again, Valdez used the powerful medium of the theater to comment upon injustice, drawing parallels from a historic event to contemporary times.

Zoot Suit opened in California to critical and public acclaim. A two-year run in Los Angeles drew Hispanics to the theater in droves. Reviews on Broadway were less stunning, however. Inevitably, a film version was demanded, and Luis Valdez was called upon to bring his

Obie, the highest honor in New York off-Broadway theater.

During its early years, El Teatro Campesino produced many worthy plays, including some penned by Valdez. The company won its first of several Los Angeles Drama Critics Awards in 1969, solidifying a reputation for quality, groundbreaking work. Touring extensively throughout Europe, it broadened its audience in the process. The mid-1970s would see a golden age of Chicano theater as various theatrical companies were formed, with El Teatro Campesino at the very center of things.

Valdez remained busy writing and directing. He also accepted a teaching work to the screen. Marking his big-screen directorial debut, Valdez cast his brother Daniel and actor Edward James Olmos as leads, essentially presenting a filmed version of the play. The approach was off-putting to some, but the performances were enthralling, and the film gained a Golden Globe nomination for Best Motion Picture from the Hollywood Foreign Press Association.

This opportunity might have signaled the launching of a film career adapting plays for the cinema, but Valdez took a different route. He instead scripted and directed 1987's *La Bamba*, a biopic of 1950s rocker Ritchie Valens. What otherwise might have remained a footnote in music history became the stuff of legend, with Valens's story receiving a fully fleshed-out treatment in Valdez's capable hands. A lesser talent might have sensationalized the script or rewritten history, but Valdez did not. His sympathetic direction brought out the best in his stars, giving a boost to the careers of actors Lou Diamond Phillips and Esai Morales. The film was a smash, as popular with critics as it was with the

public. Unexpectedly, this politically charged writer-director had created a mainstream Hollywood movie while sacrificing none of his principles.

Valdez has continued to be a presence in the film community but has sometimes worried his theater career was becoming sublimated to Hollywood's demands, sacrificing the resources he had to put into it. Whatever the challenges a film career presents, Luis Valdez's place as the father of Chicano theater is secure. He continues to write and produce plays between the occasional television film project.

Rock 'n' roll pioneer Ritchie Valens was vividly portrayed by actor Lou Diamond Phillips *(center)* in Valdez's 1987 biopic, *La Bamba.* Bolstered by a soundtrack featuring East L.A. rockers Los Lobos, the film told the story of rock's first Hispanic star.

FÉLIX FRANCISCO VARELA Y MORALES

Exiled from Cuba for relentlessly fighting for that country's independence, Father Félix Francisco Varela y Morales went to New York, where he made the city a kinder and more welcoming place for countless immigrants.

ORPHANED AT AGE SIX, Félix Fran cisco Jose Maria de la Concepcion Varela y Morales was expected to go into the army as his father and mother's families had done before him. When asked by his grandfather if he was ready to enter the military at age 14, Varela surprised the older man by replying, "I wish to be a soldier of Jesus Christ, the Lord; I do not wish to kill men but to save souls."

Born in Havana, Cuba, in 1788, Varela was a rebel from an early age. He was also a firm advocate of Cuba's need for complete independence. Ordained into the priesthood in 1811 by Bishop Diaz Espada y Landa at San Carlos Seminary, Varela immediately began to stir up trouble in his classes by insisting on teaching in Spanish, a language that tended to be ignored in academia at the time, rather than in Latin. His interests were wide: He was one of the first to write in Spanish on topics such as logic, metaphysics, and ethics; he encouraged seminaries to include courses on chem-

istry, botany, zoology, physics, math, and drawing; he helped establish the first philharmonic society in Cuba; and he was even elected to represent Cuba in Spanish parliament. But in 1823, as a result of his political beliefs and writings, he went into exile in the United States.

Varela moved to New York, where he would spend the rest of his life. That life was dedicated to helping others—he was often considered a true miracle for the endless stream of immigrants who came into the country in the early 1800s. In a time of ethnic tension and segrega-tion in the city, Varela offered his services to everyone, no matter where they came from. He became especially popular among Irish and German immigrants. He shared everything he had with them, down to his last piece of clothing. Dur-ing the cholera epidemic of 1832, he provided tremendous support for Irish immigrants. As he had in Cuba, he quickly became a spokesperson for the downtrodden. Establishing *El Habanero*, an early Spanish newspaper in the

leader Jose Marti was born. Later in his life, Marti would credit Varela as "the man who taught us how to think." Throughout Cuba, Varela's words and deeds are still famous, and he is honored by many generations.

In September 1997, the U.S. Postal Service honored Varela by creating a stamp in his image. There is also a movement within the Roman Catholic Church to grant sainthood for Father Varela. When Pope John Paul II visited Cuba for the first time in 1998, he called the priest "the father of Cuban culture" and visited his grave, revealing that he, too, prayed for Varela's canonization. On that same visit, Fidel Castro presented the Pope with a rare leather-bound edition of a 19th-century biography of the priest, one of only nine currently known to exist.

Félix Francisco Varela y Morales was the Catholic vicar general in New York City during the mid-1800s. Among many other accomplishments, he championed the rights of immigrants flooding into the city from all over the world.

United States, Varela focused his writing on tolerance, education, and immigrants' rights. He also organized parish aid societies, nurseries, and orphanages to more directly address the immediate needs of his people. He ministered to both their spiritual and physical sides.

During his time in New York, Varela served as the vicar general for the city and also established a number of churches and schools. He continued to fight for the independence of Puerto Rico and Cuba until his death. Interestingly, he died in 1853, the year Cuban

WILLIAM CARLOS WILLIAMS

A new direction was forged in American poetry in the 20th century by a man whose livelihood was healing the sick. Like playwright Anton Chekhov, William Carlos Williams was a doctor by trade. He was that rare individual who creates something new in an artistic field without actually dedicating his entire life to that pursuit on a full-time basis.

Poet William Carlos Williams made it his life's work to capture on the written page the unique flavor and rhythm of American speech. His *Paterson* series, begun in 1946, depicted the native character of Americans through his plain verse.

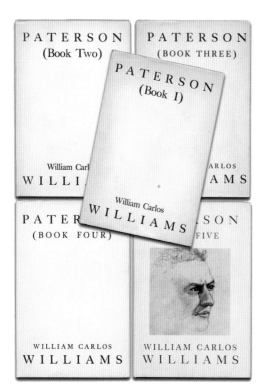

WILLIAM CARLOS WILLIAMS was born in Rutherford, New Jersey, in 1883. His father was a well-to-do Briton who came to America at the age of five, spending time in the Caribbean before eventually settling in New York City. Williams's mother was from Puerto Rico, where she met his father, and had studied painting in Paris. Though frustrated that her potential career was ended by marriage, she instilled a keen eye in her son.

Williams grew up in a home where several languages were spoken, and he would eventually attend boarding schools in Switzerland and France. His father, though often absent, would read Shakespeare to William Carlos Williams and his brother, Edward. So it was that Williams enjoyed a cultured upbringing that exposed him to a variety of international influences. It is therefore all the more striking that the dominant theme of his work would be discovering and exploring what he called "the American idiom."

At an early age, Williams decided that he would pursue both medicine *and* poetry. While attending medical school at the University of Pennsylvania, he formed lasting friendships with future literary greats Ezra Pound, Hilda Doolittle, and Marianne Moore. Williams interned in New York before completing his education in advanced pediatrics in Germany. By 1910, he had married and set up private practice in Rutherford, New Jersey.

Despite the demands of his profession, he was a prolific writer. After he had privately published one collection of poems, he produced a second, entitled *The Tempers*, which was published in London in 1913 with help from Pound. Williams would maintain a steady stream of poetry, essays, and plays throughout his career. He visited the bohemian haunts of New

Language devoid of pretension or contrived metaphor was Williams's hallmark. The deliberate plainness of his wording was deceptively simple, but it fully captured the profundity he sought to highlight within the mundane. His groundbreaking use of meter and rhythm was equally astonishing. Perhaps his finest hour came with the series entitled *Paterson*, published beginning in 1946. Here, he sought to encapsulate the whole of the American essence within the microcosm of the local.

Though Williams's reputation seemed to pale alongside contemporaries T. S. Eliot and William Butler Yeats, younger audiences were always quicker to pick up on his work. The Beats, a new generation of poets emerging in the 1950s, found kinship with him, and others saw ties going back as far as Walt Whitman. Williams died in 1963, living long enough to witness the validation of his contribution to poetry.

Though highly regarded today as a pioneering poet of free verse, during his life, Williams was professionally known to many as a doctor. He was often associated with poets such as William Butler Yeats and T. S. Eliot, but his unique voice would provide great inspiration to the Beat poets of a later generation.

York City, steeping himself in current culture and artistic developments. As his craft developed, a singular voice emerged, independent of any obvious influences.

Though he never signed on to the "Imagist Manifesto" put forth by his colleagues in an issue of *Poetry* describing the components of Modernist poetry, Williams's work was its very embodiment. The poet set about creating a uniquely American voice through his work, one that encapsulated the national experience for Americans of all backgrounds and locales. Colloquialisms were incorporated into his compositions, and he began using free verse, unfettered by artificial limitations, to describe his subjects with precision and detail.

RAÚL YZAGUIRRE

Abandoned by his parents as a small child, Raúl Yzaguirre turned aside resentment to work toward the betterment of Hispanics through the political system as head of the National Council of La Raza.

From his Dickensian childhood to his rise as one of the country's most accomplished Hispanic activists, Raúl Yzaguirre displayed enormous grit and determination in bettering the lives of his people. In 1974, he became head of the newly founded National Council of La Raza. The years he had spent in government service gave him the know-how to work the levers of power effectively.

To MOST PARENTS, a first-born child is to be treasured and revered, but poverty and deprivation can sometimes pervert natural laws. While child abuse is all too common, abandonment without explanation seems exceptionally heartless. That the child in question could move beyond any deep-seated resentments and devote a life to good works goes beyond any reasonable expectation.

Such is the beginning of Raúl Yzaguirre's story. He was born in 1939 near the Texas border town of Brownsville. When he was four, his parents packed up their car and drove him to the home of his maternal grandparents in the Rio Grande Valley of South Texas. Shortly after their arrival, the two adults got in the car and left. The trauma of this unexpected desertion devastated the sensitive boy. But while he was profoundly affected by this turn of events, circumstances forced him to develop his own resources.

Restless, Yzaguirre ran away from his grandparents' home at 13, seeking a life catching fish in Corpus Christi. That odyssey would result in a series of adventures that included hitchhiking, being questioned by the police about a murder, and an offer of adoption from a family who took him in. Arrival at his destination landed him a series of menial jobs ranging from washing dishes to removing heads from shrimp. Although he likely did not realize it, he was seeking some sort of certainty to which he could attach himself. The adolescent was ripe for finding something to believe in.

His cause arrived by chance contact with the newly formed American G.I. Forum, Hector García's political organization. Yzaguirre began attending the group's meetings, which raised his awareness of the discrimination he had long ago become used to but now no longer accepted as inevitable. Reinvigorated, the youth returned to his grandparents in San Juan to resume his education. Though still in his teens, he began organizing youth chapters of the G.I. Forum.

Following a stint in the Air Force and a flirtation with a medical career, Yzaguirre found his path within the burgeoning civil rights movement, beginning with the founding of the National Organization for Mexican American Services in 1964. Tenure with President Lyndon Johnson's Office of Economic Development provided him with invaluable insight into the workings of federal bureaucracy. The entire sum of his experiences coalesced when the Southwest Council of La Raza, the powerful grassroots Hispanic advocacy group, became the National Council of La Raza (NCLR) in 1972.

Part Washington think tank and part lobbyist, the NCLR became one of the capital's largest organizations for policy study and ethnic interests. Under Yzaguirre's leadership beginning in 1974, the organization received major funding for programs. Some of these programs included economic development in poor communities, after-school programs, and job training. His vision for what goals the group could realistically achieve, leveraged by intimate knowledge of the capabilities of federal power, helped make the NCLR's efforts most effective.

After 30 years as head of the NCLR, Yzaguirre stepped down in December 2004. In a statement announcing his retirement, he said, "I am a very fortunate man. I have had the singular honor of fighting for our people for half a century.... I have followed my passion as an advocate for my community. These things have given meaning to my life, and for that I am eternally grateful."

With Yzaguirre at its helm for three decades, the NCLR had a multipronged approach to Hispanic empowerment, which included emphasis on health, education, investment, economics, and media. Yzaguirre's ability to mobilize the troops was a powerful asset that allowed the group to prosper even after his retirement in 2004.

INDEX